Nations in the News
INDIA

By David Wilson

MASON CREST
Philadelphia · Miami

Mason Crest
450 Parkway Drive, Suite D
Broomall, PA 19008
(866) MCP-BOOK (toll free)
www.masoncrest.com

Copyright © 2020 by Mason Crest, an imprint of National Highlights, Inc. All rights reserved. No part of this publication may be reproduced or transmitted in any form or by any means, electronic or mechanical, including photocopying, recording, taping, or any information storage and retrieval system, without permission in writing from the publisher.

Printed in the United States of America.

First printing
9 8 7 6 5 4 3 2 1

Series ISBN: 978-1-4222-4242-1
Hardcover ISBN: 978-1-4222-4245-2
ebook ISBN: 978-1-4222-7573-3

Cataloging-in-Publication Data is available on file
at the Library of Congress.

Developed and Produced by Print Matters Productions, Inc.
(www.printmattersinc.com)

Cover and Interior Design by Tom Carling, Carling Design Inc.

QR CODES AND LINKS TO THIRD-PARTY CONTENT
You may gain access to certain third-party content ("third-party sites") by scanning and using the QR Codes that appear in this publication (the "QR Codes"). We do not operate or control in any respect any information, products, or services on such third-party sites linked to by us via the QR Codes included in this publication, and we assume no responsibility for any materials you may access using the QR Codes. Your use of the QR Codes may be subject to terms, limitations, or restrictions set forth in the applicable terms of use or otherwise established by the owners of the third-party sites. Our linking to such third-party sites via the QR Codes does not imply an endorsement or sponsorship of such third-party sites, or the information, products, or services offered on or through the third-party sites, nor does it imply an endorsement or sponsorship of this publication by the owners of such third-party sites.

Contents

Introduction 6
1 Security Issues 20
2 Government and Politics 36
3 Economy 52
4 Quality of Life 70
5 Society and Culture 88
Series Glossary of Key Terms 100
Chronology of Key Events 105
Further Reading & Internet Resources 107
Index 108
Author's Biography 111
Credits 112

KEY ICONS TO LOOK FOR

Words to Understand: These words with their easy-to-understand definitions will increase the reader's understanding of the text while building vocabulary skills.

Sidebars: This boxed material within the main text allows readers to build knowledge, gain insights, explore possibilities, and broaden their perspectives by weaving together additional information to provide realistic and holistic perspectives.

Educational Videos: Readers can view videos by scanning our QR codes, providing them with additional educational content to supplement the text.

Text-Dependent Questions: These questions send the reader back to the text for more careful attention to the evidence presented there.

Research Projects: Readers are pointed toward areas of further inquiry connected to each chapter. Suggestions are provided for projects that encourage deeper research and analysis.

Series Glossary of Key Terms: This back-of-the-book glossary contains terminology used throughout this series. Words found here increase the reader's ability to read and comprehend higher-level books and articles in this field.

The Lotus Temple, located in Delhi, is a Baha'i house of worship.

India at a Glance

Total Land Area	1,269,219 square miles
Climate	Various, from tropical monsoon in south to temperate in north
Natural Resources	Coal, iron ore, manganese, mica, bauxite, rare earth elements, titanium ore, chromite, natural gas, diamonds, petroleum, limestone, arable land
Land Use	Agricultural land: 60.5 percent (52.8 percent arable land, 4.2 percent permanent crops, 3.5 percent permanent pasture); forest: 23.1 percent; other: 16.4 percent
Urban Population	34 percent of total population (2018)
Major Urban Areas	New Delhi (28.514 million); Mumbai (19.98 million); Kolkata (14.681 million); Bangalore (11.44 million); Chennai (10.456 million); Hyderabad (9.482 million)
Geography	Southern Asia, bordering the Arabian Sea and the Bay of Bengal, between Burma and Pakistan

Introduction

The name India evokes the mythical, the exotic, and the tranquil: images of elephants lumbering through cities, of ancient ruins thousands of years old, of holy men at prayer in shrines, and of endless fields of jade-green rice paddies. The Republic of India features all of these things but much more as well: It is a nation of conflict, of growth and opportunity, and of desperate poverty and tremendous challenges. It is a nation with many friends but no allies, and a nation with many ideas but few chances for change.

India is the dominant feature of southern Asia. It is often called the **subcontinent**, because its geography only recently linked up with Asia itself, colliding with the mainland about 25 million years ago and creating the drastic upthrust of the Himalaya Mountains. India is the seventh-largest nation in the world, coming in at 1.2 million square miles, making it about twice as large as Alaska. The historic range of India has at times been larger or smaller than its current boundaries; some empires like the Mughal controlled much of Pakistan in addition to India. Its current boundaries, set by the British Empire's geographers, were an attempt to partition Southern Asia in a fashion that would be favorable to Muslims in Pakistan as well as Hindus in India.

Words to Understand

Caste: Ethnic social hierarchy of India, dating to ancient times, forming restrictive classes of peoples.

Debt bondage: Partial or total servitude for the purposes of paying off debts.

Industrialization: The transition from an agricultural economy to a manufacturing economy.

Insurgency: An active revolt or uprising against the authorities.

Subcontinent: A geographic area smaller than an individual continent but larger than most nations.

Bikers ride through the Himalayas.

A few numbers help to illustrate the sheer size of India. With 1.3 billion people, only China has a higher population; the four next-largest nations combined do not equal India's size. One in five people worldwide is Indian. This huge population resides in a small space, most of it along the coastal regions and in the Ganges River Valley of the north; some parts of India, especially the western deserts, have almost no population at all.

India's climate varies by location. It is predominantly known for its tropical climate, because most of the country lies within a few hundred miles of the equator. The eastern half of the country is hot and rainy, enjoying the annual monsoon storms in the summer months that dump huge quantities of water throughout the country, providing the moisture needed for intensive agricultural production. The western half is far drier, most notably the Thar Desert of Rajasthan at the border with Pakistan. This region receives little rain, creating the world's 17th-largest desert. Despite the lack of rain for agriculture, sheep herding in this region produces about

Nations in the News:  **INDIA**

IN THE NEWS
Population Growth

Just one in three Indians lives in cities, but India's huge base population means that its urban population is larger than the populations of the United States and Canada combined. Urbanization has followed **industrialization** in typical patterns as rural workers migrate to cities in search of better pay, living conditions, and job opportunities. This trend has not been entirely positive: Slums have grown throughout Indian cities wherever they could not absorb the migrant population, leading to filthy and crowded living conditions for the poorest of the poor. This population shift has also produced pollution, fierce traffic snarls, and exploitation of inexpensive labor.

By 2050, more Indians may live in cities than in rural areas; if they do, India will have the largest population shift of rural-to-urban in human history. India's largest cities are located through the Ganges River Valley of the north and the coastal areas of the south. The central regions contain fewer cities, although they are dotted by thousands upon thousands of individual towns and villages.

A crowded city street in Mumbai.

A sheep herder leads his flock through the snowy terrain of the Himalaya Mountains.

Learn about a geographical feature of India.

half of all Indian wool. In the far northern regions, the mighty Himalayas produce a temperate mountain climate: Heavy snowfall results in glaciers and river formations, whereas the cooler temperatures make for attractive tourist destinations.

Nations in the News: INDIA

Most of the surface of India is dotted with farms, millions or even hundreds of millions strong, because two-thirds of its population lives in rural areas and works in agriculture. India has the second-largest swath of arable land in the entire world, a full 50 percent of its entire land area, trailing only the United States. This vast land area allows India to grow food not only for its own population but also for export to the wider world. Because of the huge population, 12 percent of the total land in India is taken up by urban development.

The history of India is tremendously long and complex, equal to the history of China or Europe in its scale and depth. The first civilizations appeared around the rivers flowing from the Himalayas to the Indian Ocean some 5,000 years ago. They developed the languages, social structures, and religions that form the base of contemporary Indian society. Conquests by foreign powers further diversified Southern Asia, culminating in the British Raj of 1857,

A group of women work in a rice field.

when all of India, Pakistan, and Bangladesh became part of the larger British Empire. India won independence in 1947, promptly began fighting several of its neighbors, instituted a vast number of government offices to manage the huge population, and emerged in the twenty-first century as perhaps the most powerful nation in the Southern Hemisphere.

India today earns headlines primarily for its economic growth. It is in the midst of a major economic boom, enjoying annual growth of 5 to 10 percent, far higher than any Western nation. India's economy has grown fivefold since 1970, and today India is the sixth-largest economy in the entire world according to the World Bank, reflecting the adoption of new technologies and the impact of India's growing industries. Industrialization in India has made rapid progress, and economists agree that India will be one of the wealthiest nations in the world in the immediate future. India has followed the track of China as first a manufacturing power and then an information-technology power. It is clear that these two nations will be the dominant power players in Asia, although it is not yet clear whether they can peacefully cooperate or whether friction between them will create future conflict.

India's new wealth has increased the quality of life for many, yet it has not spread across the nation like the annual monsoon winds. The growth of the Indian middle class is steady but slow. Half of the population of India still works on farms as their ancestors might have done thousands of years ago; all but a few percent work in the unorganized sector, where they may earn as little as two dollars per day in tasks ranging from street sweeping to street peddling. Hundreds of millions of Indians live in rural areas without access to electricity or fresh water, and millions more live in such desperate poverty that they are chronically hungry, reduced to begging or stealing to get by.

India is not a wealthy nation in most natural resources, lacking enough oil and natural gas for national self-sufficiency. It does feature an abundance of both coal and iron, yet these two resources are considered relatively low quality, and India must import both coal briquettes and finished steel for use in its

industries. Most of India's remaining forests are protected, but in parts of the country (especially the poorer and less dense northeast) forestry and mining are more common. With relatively few precious metals but a much greater quantity of precious gems, India imports a large amount of gold and silver and exports a great deal of finished jewelry.

Indian poverty remains entrenched throughout society yet illustrates the progress of the government in recent decades. Thirty years ago, India looked like a very different nation: Only a small segment of the population had any education and could read; infant mortality ranked far lower, but births per woman ranked far higher; almost 90 percent of the population lived on rural farms; and India's secondary and tertiary sectors barely existed to provide better jobs to workers at all.

Children of the slums in Bihar.

From the outside, India appears to be a nation of peace. After fighting three wars with neighboring Pakistan and one war with China, all over the issue of national borders set by the former British colonizers, it has managed to largely quell the **insurgency** in Kashmir. This province in the northwest has been effectively split between Pakistan and India (reflecting a Muslim-Hindu divide in the population, respectively) after armed conflict and peace treaties failed to provide either nation with control of the entire region as they desire.

India has shot up the ranks to become one of the global leaders in military spending despite having no formal alliances with any other nation. Today, India projects power throughout South Asia and the Indian Ocean. Its rivalry with Pakistan has evolved into a nuclear rivalry, because both nations have these weapons of mass destruction. Moments of great tension between these two unfriendly neighbors have called into question whether either side will use them.

For the vast majority of Indians, nuclear war with Pakistan is a faraway thought. Most Indians instead must focus on the here and now: how to get a better job, get more food for their family, ensure their children get an education, and keep the traditions of the past in an ever-changing world. Indian society features many traditionalist elements, dating back centuries or even millennia, all of which can potentially create friction when contrasted with idealized notions of a secular, democratic, and equal society. Issues like the **caste** system, **debt bondage**, abuse of women, child labor, religious strife, and poor public health must all be addressed before Indian citizens can enjoy the freedoms and benefits of the modern world. With hundreds of millions of people living below the global benchmarks for poverty, India has few solutions to a wide variety of problems.

One great challenge lies in India's tremendous diversity. Hundreds of languages, ethnicities, and religious practices divide a single country into a vast array of individual cultures. Each state of India (29 in total) may have people, religions, and languages unrecognizable to its neighbors. Indian census data create the

A City of Contrasts

Kolkata, or Calcutta, on the eastern coast, is a city of contrasts. Called the "City of Joy," it is home to huge numbers of urban poor. Mother Teresa famously set up her charities and missionaries to bring relief to the many people of Kolkata who could not afford food, clothes, or medicine. Many symbols of national history and culture, including the Indian Museum, the National Library, and the Academy of Fine Arts, are located in Kolkata.

image of a largely unified nation with just two major ethnic groups, yet this belies the far greater degree to which India is fragmented. These ethnic divisions reflect differences in caste, religion, and earnings, which in turn keep parts of Indian society in competition with others. At a time when the national government increasingly caters to the Hindu majority, the rights and privileges of India's many, many minorities will create complexity in a nation that overflows with problems—some of them dating back to the colonial era.

One major problem that, unlike hunger and poverty, has not carried over from the colonial era is pollution. Indian cities are among the worst polluted in the entire world today because gridlock traffic and coal-fired power plants emit vast amounts of CO_2 into the atmosphere. Just as India has climbed to be a top nation in population and wealth, it has also climbed to become the world's third-largest emitter of carbon. The tremendous pollution to major cities has shed years from average life expectancies. Visitors are warned not to visit cities like Mumbai or Delhi unless the winds are strong enough to shift the smog and allow for a fresh breath. Pollution to rivers, like the holy Ganges, imperils the main source of water for most of the population. Deforestation has reduced the habitat available for India's charismatic megafauna, like elephants, rhinos, and tigers.

India continues to struggle with reducing air and water pollution.

India has many friends and good relations throughout the world, aside from its immediate neighbor, Pakistan, and represents a major trade partner to the modern economy, with partnerships around the globe and a great deal of foreign interest in its newfound growth. Indian products ranging from produce to clothing to vehicles end up for sale in dozens of countries worldwide. Its commitments to the United Nations, including providing the second-largest number of peacekeepers of any nation, have given it a great deal of credibility and good standing in the international community. It remains to be seen how India will manage this good standing: Its application for a permanent seat on the UN Security Council, giving it veto power over UN initiatives, would cement India's position as a global power. With many friends but no true allies, India may face an uphill battle to be considered a great power.

Text-Dependent Questions

1. Which country has a higher population than India?

2. In what year did India gain its independence from the British Empire?

3. How many states are there in India?

Research Project

Research one of the major religions practiced in India. Write a brief summary of its history (including whether it was founded in India), beliefs, holidays, and important sacred books or texts. Include information on how the religion is being practiced in India today.

An Indian army checkpoint in the contested region of Kashmir.

India in the News in the 21st Century

2017 "Exceptional" for India Department of Atomic Energy
World Nuclear News, August 20, 2018

India Court Upholds 2012 Dehli Gang Rapists' Death Penalty
BBC, May 5, 2017

Just the Job: Ever More Indians Are Struggling to Find Work
The Economist, September 24, 2017

Caste in India: Backward Ho!
The Economist, February 27, 2016

Not Just a Game: India and Pakistan's Cricketing Rivalry Has Always Been about More Than Sport
The Economist, March 21, 2016

India Plants 50 Million Trees in One Day
National Geographic, July 18, 2016

Kashmir: Reviving the Cause
The Economist, August 11, 2016

India's Armed Forces: Guns and Ghee
The Economist, September 22, 2016

Indian Government Declares Delhi Air Quality Pollution an Emergency
The Guardian, November 6, 2016

MDG Report 2014: India among Worst Performers in Poverty Reduction, Maternal Death, and Sanitation
Down to Earth, July 4, 2015

Indian Election Result: 2014 Is Modi's Year as BJP Secures Victory
The Guardian, May 16, 2014

Chapter 1

Security Issues

It is appropriate that the two national symbols of the Republic of India are the elephant and the tiger: On the one hand, India's bureaucracy is often compared to a lumbering elephant. On the other hand, its military evokes the tiger's ferocity: India's armed forces are highly advanced, very large, and capable of maintaining order throughout the broader Indian Ocean.

Conflicts

The core principle of revered Indian leader Mahatma Gandhi's resistance to British occupation of India was nonviolence. In many ways the Indian government has striven to live up to this ideal: declaring itself neutral during the Cold War (and the resulting rivalry today between the United States and Russia), working to

Words to Understand

Asylum: Political protection from enemies, often achieved by fleeing to another country.

Cease-fire: A reduction in hostility during a conflict when both sides agree not to fight, possibly but not necessarily ending a war.

Gross domestic product: The sum total of value created by a national economy, reflecting the output of all work.

Paramilitary: A semi-militarized force, trained in tactics and organized by rank, but not officially part of a nation's formal military.

20 Nations in the News:  INDIA

India's military marches in a parade in celebration of Independence Day.

India's Security Issues at a Glance

Military Size	5,077,050 total personnel
Military Service	16–18 years of age for volunteer military service; no conscription
Military Branches	Indian Army, Indian Navy, Indian Air Force, Indian Coast Guard
Military Spending	2.47 percent of GDP (2016)
Active Terrorist Groups (home-based)	Hizbul Mujhaideen, Indian Mujahedeen, Islamic State of Iraq and al-Sham
Active Terrorist Groups (international)	al-Qaeda, Harakat ul-Jihad-i-Islami, Harakat ul-Mujahidin, Jaish-e-Mohammad, Lashkar-e-Taiba, Liberation Tigers of Tamil Eelam
Illicit Drugs	World's largest producer of licit opium for the pharmaceutical trade, with an undetermined quantity of opium diverted to illicit international drug markets

Mahatma Gandhi was a force for peaceful change.

build good relationships with humanitarian aid and missions, and endeavoring to be a global leader. Yet the strength of the Indian military speaks louder than any politician, and the nation's own history is not without major conflicts.

Many wars in history result from disagreements between neighbors, and India is no outlier to this phenomenon. The Republic of India has fought wars against only two nations, Pakistan and China, both on account of disagreements over territory and borders. Like many conflicts in the modern world, many of India's disagreements with its neighbors can be traced to colonial powers dividing up the map as they saw fit, paying little (if any) attention to the inhabitants of these places, their beliefs, their cultures, or their ability to live peacefully with others.

Kashmir and Pakistan

The roots of India's conflicts lie in her independence from Britain in 1947. National independence for India came at the same time as it did for Pakistan. The British hoped to divide the Asian subcontinent between a primarily Muslim majority in Pakistan and a primarily Hindu majority in India. Jammu and Kashmir, a princely state in the northern region of the two nations' border (often referred to simply as Kashmir), was given the decision about which nation it would rather join. The Kashmiri authorities wavered, however, and neither India nor Pakistan decided it would allow this major decision to be taken out of its own hands.

The first conflict of the Republic of India's history began just weeks after independence. The Indo-Pakistani War of 1947–1948 lasted a little over a year and saw relatively few fatalities—just 6,000 dead on Pakistan's side and 1,000 on India's side—but wracked the Kashmir valley with violence. Pakistan believed it had the right to rule the Muslims living in the region; India believed the official lines drawn after independence ceded the region to its authority.

A group of Indian soldiers await orders during the war in 1947.

The war ended with a UN-brokered **cease-fire**, ineffective in solving the core issue but effective enough to buy limited peace in the region, keeping the northern region in Pakistani authority and the southern region in Indian authority.

India's rivalry with Pakistan only intensified over time. In 1965, Pakistan sent a larger group of soldiers to infiltrate Kashmir, accelerate the insurgency, and wrest control of the region away from India. India declared full-scale war, leading to a 17-day conflict that, at the time, was the largest engagement of tanks in a battle since World War II. A second cease-fire, again brokered by the UN, came after both nations' militaries lost about 3,000 soldiers, over 200 tanks, and several dozen aircraft each. Little territory changed hands as a result of the cease-fire, and the central issue of ownership of this remote region remained unchanged.

A third war with Pakistan was, perhaps surprisingly, not fought over Kashmir at all. Instead, India supported Bangladesh (previously East Pakistan) in its revolution and independence movement, leading to the third Indo-Pakistani War, fought in 1971. Although this war was one of the shortest in all of history, lasting just 13 days, it was nevertheless the bloodiest conflict in the rivalry between the two neighbors. Pakistan lost about 9,000 soldiers, along with about a dozen naval vessels and 75 airplanes. India endured less hardship, with about 4,000 dead, two lost ships, and 45 airplanes. More importantly, Bangladesh became an independent nation, one enjoying good relations with India.

The divide between pro-Pakistan Muslims and pro-Indian Hindus in Kashmir continues to this day: Further wars have followed in Kashmir, along with casual violence, terrorism, and murders outside of organized combat. Perhaps half of India's entire armed forces operate today in Kashmir, quelling the Muslim insurgency with mixed results. Most diplomats and politicians believe that, if given the option, Kashmiris would vote for independence rather than rule from either Pakistan or India. This choice, unfortunately, is almost certainly beyond their reach. To make matters worse, China has also claimed territory in Kashmir. The end result is that a Google Maps search for Kashmir reveals different lines of control depending from which of the three countries the search is performed.

China

For thousands of years, Indian and Chinese civilizations have had little to fear from one another, separated as they are by the Tibetan Plateau and the highest mountains in the world. Good fences make good neighbors, but in the industrial era, even the tallest mountains are not enough to keep two nations from friction and mistrust.

Throughout the 1950s, both India and China enjoyed rising stars and became power players in Asia. They share a difference of opinion, however, about a variety of topics, perhaps none more important than their border and the status of Tibet, the region of southern China. The Chinese believe Tibet to be an integral component of the broader Chinese nation, whereas India (and many other members of the world) believes Tibet ought to be an independent nation.

When India offered **asylum** to the leader of Tibetan independence, the Dalai Lama, after the 1959 Tibetan uprising against Chinese rule, a number of border skirmishes broke out between the Indian military and the Chinese military. Disputes over borders boiled into outright conflict in 1962 after disagreement about the placement of the McMahon Line, a colonial-era line drawn on the map between the two nations. The war lasted just a month and a day as the overwhelmingly stronger Chinese army pushed forward into Indian territory before withdrawing to its stated zone of control, then agreeing to a cease-fire. It was one of the few wars in history confined entirely to high altitudes, as well as one of the few wars in the twentieth century where both nations' navies and air forces could not play a part in the fighting.

Mistrust between India and China has waxed and waned in the decades since the 1962 Sino-Indian War. India looked to support from China against conflicts with Pakistan; Pakistan today is ironically one of China's strongest allies in Central Asia. The Chinese-Indian rivalry has since largely cooled, especially because both nations have rapidly growing economies and rely on each other as major trade partners.

Nuclear Weapons

Military losses on the battlefield by both India and Pakistan, however, may pale in comparison to the next stage in their rivalry: the acquisition of nuclear weapons. India began its nuclear weapons program in 1967, a result of the second Indo-Pakistani War as well as the 1962 border war with China. In fact, Indian politicians demonstrated an enthusiasm for a nuclear weapons program in the earliest days of the history of the Republic: Jawaharlal Nehru, the nation's first prime minister, said in 1946 that India in the atomic age would defend herself "by all means at her disposal."

By 1974, India successfully tested its first nuclear weapon, Smiling Buddha, making it the first nonaligned nation (that is, neither communist nor a member of the North Atlantic Treaty Organization (NATO), an international military alliance) to acquire nuclear weapons. India has a policy of no first use, meaning it will not use nuclear weapons themselves in any conflict unless an enemy has already used them against India. India has a nuclear triad, meaning the ability to deliver nuclear weapons by sea, by air, or by strategic missiles.

Pakistan, easily reading the writing on the wall, launched its own nuclear program in retaliation; Zulfikar Ali Bhutto, prime minister of Pakistan from 1973 to 1977, famously said that the Pakistani people would eat grass if they had to in order to realize a nuclear weapon of their own. Pakistan successfully tested its own nuclear bomb in 1998.

India today has missiles that can launch a nuclear warhead anywhere in Asia, Africa, or Europe, and is believed to have the equivalent amount of plutonium needed for 1,000 bombs. Pakistan, by contrast, is believed to have the equivalent needed for about 150 bombs. Many diplomats, military strategists, and politicians question whether nuclear war is more likely between Pakistan and India than it is between the United States and Russia or China.

Alliances

India is a unique global power in that it has no formal military alliances. It was a founding member of the Non-Aligned Movement in 1961, a membership of 120 nations that have no major military alliance with any of the global powers (usually referring to the United States, European Union, Russian Federation, and sometimes China).

India, however, does have a number of friends. It is part of many economic agreements, including the Asian Development Bank and the G20, giving it the ability to exert its financial might and win over disagreements or woo potential trade partners. It is also currently the second-largest provider of peacekeeping forces to the UN.

The Indian Army displays Agni II, a medium-range ballistic missile, at a parade.

IN THE NEWS

A. Q. Khan

One of the most fascinating stories of India's nuclear rivalry with Pakistan is the story of how Pakistan acquired nuclear technology in the first place. It all depended on one man, Abdul Qadeer (A. Q.) Khan, sometimes called a real-life James Bond villain, who literally pocketed nuclear plans and walked out the front door. He then built a network throughout the Middle East of nuclear buyers and sellers.

India is a leading global buyer and seller of military hardware, happy to purchase from the United States, France, Israel, Great Britain, and Russia. India's good relations with many of these nations, in fact, is a reflection of its eagerness to buy hundreds of millions of dollars' worth of military goods, from rifles to aircraft.

India has signed many treaties of cooperation and friendship, including one with the Soviet Union in 1971. However, it has not signed military treaties with neighbors or major powers, preferring instead to project its own influence over Southern Asia directly.

Regional Relations

India boasts the largest economy and military presence in the entire Indian Ocean. Its ability to exert power and influence events from Australia to Madagascar reflects its commitment to becoming a global power, as well as its good ties with most of its neighbors (besides, of course, Pakistan). India also serves in a sort of caretaker role for some of the small nations on its periphery, like Sri Lanka, Nepal, and Bhutan, providing military protection, infrastructure, and trade, even though disagreements between India and these neighbors do exist.

Regional relations for India are complicated by the aggressive expansion of Chinese diplomatic, economic, and military power. China views itself as the dominant power in Asia for the twenty-first century and has stepped up its role as friend and ally to many nations in Central and South Asia, creating zones of influence that India itself may not be able to bridge. As an example, China's One Belt, One Road policy provides a huge number of soft loans, transportation paths, construction projects, and electrification grids throughout Asia, hoping to rebuild the Silk Road of antiquity with Chinese economic and political power as the central tenet. This project is not specifically targeted at India but nevertheless has established China as a better friend to many Asian nations, even those who might otherwise come under India's direct sphere of influence.

International Relations

India is a well-known and largely well-respected power in the international community. As India has reformed its economy and politics, it has provided a contrast to rival Pakistan, which continues to funnel money toward a corrupt military. This situation has given India a great deal of favorable recognition, especially over the situation in Kashmir. However, India's handling of the Kashmir situation has brought about a great deal of criticism.

There are further questions about India's nuclear weapons and its commitment to nuclear peace. India tested a second nuclear weapon in the late 1990s, partially in reaction to Pakistan's own nuclear test, bringing down major international sanctions. These sanctions lasted only until 2001, however, when the September 11 attacks suddenly thrust Indian counterterrorism operations into a favorable light. India's efforts to combat the growth of al-Qaeda

in Pakistan and Afghanistan long predate American and NATO efforts to stop the terrorist cell; Indian intelligence on al-Qaeda's operations continues to assist operations in Afghanistan today.

India has also held bilateral counterterrorism training exercises with the United States and European Union, enriching its standing as well as its economy, because these major powers conducted more trade with India after relations warmed. What's more, the Indian government has made many strides to be a positive member of the nuclear community, signing on to the Missile Technology Control Regime to prevent the illicit spread of missile technology. It is also seeking entry into the Nuclear Suppliers Group, an international organization dedicated to preventing the proliferation of the material needed for the construction of nuclear arms.

One of the largest issues facing India on the global stage today is its participation in the United Nations. India, along with Japan, Germany, and Brazil, wishes to gain a permanent seat on the UN Security Council. This would bring the total number of seats on the Security Council to nine (today's members are the United States, United Kingdom, France, Russia, and China) and, more importantly, give India veto power over UN resolutions. This veto power is hugely important: As just a few examples, the United States has used veto power to quash sanctions against Israel for its treatment

The U.S. and Indian armies train together to familiarize themselves with INSAS, a type of rifle.

of Palestinians, whereas Russia has used veto power to keep ally Bashar al-Assad's government propped up in Syria.

India and its fellows face an uphill battle to claim a permanent UN Security Council seat. Perhaps surprisingly, four of the five permanent seat-holders (with the exception of China) are willing to admit India and dilute their authority. However, an international partnership dedicated to preventing expansion of the permanent Security Council, called Uniting for Consensus, wishes to keep the number of permanent seats at five. Many of the countries in these groups are economic and military rivals of India, Japan, Germany, and Brazil: Pakistan is a core member of Uniting for Consensus and doubtless fears the prospect of its powerful neighbor gaining veto power at the UN.

Human Trafficking

Despite its illegality throughout the nation, human trafficking is without a doubt one of the greatest issues facing India. Although the numbers are not absolute, India's huge size makes it the likely global leader in human trafficking; it is not an exaggeration to put the number of affected people in the millions. However, trafficking in India does not strictly involve the ongoing conflict in Kashmir. Instead, it reflects a wide range of problems central to Indian culture and economics: many factories and businesses that are in need of

Women march in solidarity with the children of India. Human trafficking—especially the exploitation of children—is a main concern.

Children working inside a brick factory.

ultra-cheap labor; the culture of debt bondage that can make people sell themselves or their family into slavery; a society that emphasizes the importance of marriage and having children above perhaps all else; and the recruitment of child soldiers.

India is currently a "tier-two watch list nation" for human trafficking, according to the U.S. State Department's *Trafficking in Persons Report*. This means it is not as bad as failed states like nearby Myanmar yet is routinely failing to meet the challenge of eliminating trafficking within as well as into and out of India. In every aspect of Indian human trafficking, it is the lowest-caste members, the *Dalit*, who bear the heaviest burdens of kidnapping, sale of people, or forced marriage. Indians from rural communities, religious or ethnic minorities, and other excluded groups are also at the highest risk of trafficking.

Most (but by no means all) trafficking in India involves debt bondage. Much as debtors in colonial America could be imprisoned, modern debtors in India have the option to sell themselves or their family members into bondage to repay the money. Furthermore, debt bondage can be passed down through generations, meaning that the people bought and sold as effective slaves to work in rice fields, brick kilns, or sweatshops may one day work alongside their children. This bondage also is responsible for selling men, women, and children overseas: Although 90 percent of India's trafficking is internal, a huge number of people are shipped to neighboring countries for work and exploitation.

Another major sector involves the sex and wedding trade. India's gender imbalance is not nearly as harsh as that of China's, yet there are still not enough brides in India for every potential husband. Indian society emphasizes the importance of building and continuing the family, resulting in social norms that are often at odds with Indian law. For example, 50 percent of all Indian women between the ages of 20 to 24 are estimated to have been married prior to the legal age. Human trafficking for forced marriage in India is relatively common today, with patterns of trafficking reflecting movement from the rural to the urban. These women are also sold as brides outside of India itself.

Those women not involved in forced marriages may be forced to enter the sex trade: Prostitution is legal throughout India, with an estimated half a million women selling sex. Organized prostitution (such as brothels or pimping) is illegal, but there is no doubt that much human trafficking feeds organized criminal and/or sex trade rings; many major cities and police departments look the other way. The Sonagachi red-light district in Kolkata has perhaps 10,000 prostitutes alone. Such prostitution, in conjunction with the need for other sex workers like dancers or bar girls, results in the trafficking of women and girls throughout India.

The problem of prostitution in India.

Illicit Drugs

As is prevalent in many contemporary terrorist organizations, militancy in Kashmir is supported by drug money. Huge quantities of opium are grown throughout northern India, Pakistan, and neighboring Afghanistan. Some of it is in fact legal (India is the world's leading supplier of medical opium), but much goes toward heroin

The poppy flower produces the drug opium. Although opium can be used legally for medicinal use, it can be used illegally as heroin, adding to the growing global epidemic.

production, which fuels addiction around the entire globe. The year 2016 saw no fewer than 608 criminal cases against drug smugglers, including 65 kilograms of seized heroin and about 500 kilograms of seized cannabis. Kashmir itself is not a center for narcotics production; instead, virtually all drugs are smuggled across the Line of Control that separates territorial claims of India from those of Pakistan. The director general of police said in 2018 that drug use represented a greater threat in Kashmir than terrorism itself.

India's drug policy officially outlaws many narcotics despite the long history of their use in Indian medicine. Cannabis, for example, has been used in India for 4,000 years, both medically and recreationally: A popular cannabis milkshake called *bhang* is central to the spring festival of Holi. The holy Vedic texts even address hemp with a prayer: "May it deliver us from woe." Today, cannabis flowers are illegal in India, although seeds and leaves can be purchased without issue. In fact, a gram of cannabis in India costs just 10 cents, one of the lowest price tags in the entire world.

Military

India's military spending as a percentage of **gross domestic product** (GDP) has barely shifted since 1960, rising from 2 percent to 2.5 percent in the span of 50 years. The great change in India's economy, however, means that one-fortieth of the national finances has become a vastly larger number. India today has the fifth-largest military budget of any nation, behind only the United States, China, Saudi Arabia, and Russia. With 1.5 million active personnel, India's military is second in size only to China, which also makes it the largest volunteer army in the world. When considering reserve and **paramilitary** personnel, India's military is not only the largest in the world but almost as large as those of China and the United States combined.

India is a major buyer and seller of arms, although the inventory numbers do not make it seem balanced. Importing $42 billion in arms per year, India then turns around and sells about $300 million per year. More impressive than the number, however, is the list of nations India sells to, including many countries in Central Asia, on the opposite border of Pakistan, and many that surround the Indian Ocean. These sales help to project Indian military power without the need for formal alliances.

A great deal of India's military is becoming homegrown as Indian aeronautical, shipbuilding, and engineering firms catch up to the biggest names on the international market. The Vikrant-class aircraft carrier, the world's first not built by a member of NATO or the former Communist Bloc, is expected to be in commission by 2020.

Terrorist Groups

Violence in Kashmir hit a high-water mark in the late 1990s and has steadily declined since then. Rising prosperity and a major peacekeeping operation by the Indian military have helped to minimize the spread, and the impact, of terrorism. More than 1,700 civilians died in fighting throughout the region in 1996; by 2013 that number fell to just 81.

Nevertheless, many challenges remain. Most terrorist groups are jihadi Islamist organizations: One of the largest, Jaise-e-Mohammed, means "Army of Mohammed," whereas Lashkar-e-Taiba means "Amry of the Pure." Many have ideological, if not official, ties with broader Islamist groups like al-Qaeda. However, support for hardline Islamic policies is not high throughout Kashmir, even in Muslim-majority areas, and few Islamist groups have proven successful at retaining high numbers of followers in the area. Many of these groups maintain other cells throughout India itself, as demonstrated by the 2001

terrorist attack against the Indian parliament building and the 2008 Mumbai shootings that left more than 174 dead.

India has been facing the risk of terrorism since its first days as an independent nation. The current counterterrorism force is one of the strongest in the world but also one of the most criticized; human rights abuse accusations against Indian security forces in Kashmir include murder, torture, and rape.

Text-Dependent Questions

1. Which national authority do most Muslims in Kashmir support or prefer to support?
2. In what ways is China a rival of India?
3. What is one major reason why India desires a permanent seat on the United Nations?

Research Project

The partitions of India and Pakistan were originally the result of British Empire surveyors. Conduct research about the survey process that divided India and Pakistan. Who made the most important decisions? What evidence supported these decisions? Write a brief report summarizing your findings.

Government and Politics

The greatest legacy of the Republic of India's time as a British colony lies in its laws and politics, some of which are totally unchanged from the British model established over a century ago. Today, India is by far the world's largest democracy, with hundreds of millions of voters turning out for national elections. The Indian government features multiparty control of both local and national politics, a system of comprehensive checks and balances, and a constitution safeguarding rights of its citizenry.

Government Type

As its name suggests, the Republic of India is indeed a republic: Its government uses the **parliamentary** model of legislature to create

Words to Understand

Commonwealth: An association of independent nations that were previously under the rule of the British Empire.

Nationalism: Ideology of high value and respect for a person's birth nation, with different forms in different countries but often promoted by governments.

Parliamentary: Governmental structure in which executive power is awarded to a cabinet of legislative body members rather than elected by the people directly.

Sovereignty: The ability of one's own country to rule itself; often used in conjunction with independence.

Voters show off their ink mark applied to their index fingers. After voting, each person applies this ink mark to their finger as a symbol of democratic privilege.

India's Government and Legal System at a Glance

Independence	August 15, 1947 (from the United Kingdom)
National Holiday	Republic Day, January 26
National Symbol(s)	The Lion Capital of Ashoka, Bengal tiger, lotus flower
Constitution	Adopted November 26, 1949, effective January 26, 1950
Legal System	Common-law system based on the English model; separate personal law codes apply to Hindus, Muslims, and Christians
Voting Eligibility	18 years of age; universal

The front of the parliament building in New Delhi includes an inscription that reads, "Liberty will not descend to a people, a people must raise themselves to Liberty, it is a blessing that must be earned before it can be enjoyed."

law and to elect the cabinet to carry out executive functions. It is a federation, meaning a governing entity of many individual states: India has 29 states and seven territories. Unlike unitary governments where the central authority dictates what powers will be devolved to localities, India's federation government does not have more power than its local governments. The national government functions from New Delhi, the country's capital and second-largest city.

India's parliamentary government reflects its association with the broader British **Commonwealth**. Many Commonwealth states, from Canada to South Africa to Australia, all utilize the parliamentary model either fully or in conjunction with a presidential model. Many have made adaptations to the basic policies, and India is no different: It has a president to serve as the head of state and head of the armed forces, separating this power from that of the prime minister.

With a budget of about $330 billion, India's government is the fifth-largest spender on the planet; relative to the scale of its population, however, its per capita government spending is just below Mexico's.

Nations in the News:  INDIA

Constitution

The constitution of India lays out the freedoms given to its people and the laws delegated to both national and local jurisdiction. It establishes constitutional supremacy, rather than parliamentary supremacy, because it was not drafted by the parliament itself. The text of the constitutional preamble draws heavily on the notions of the French Enlightenment, declaring justice, liberty, equality, and fraternity among all its citizenry.

The story of drafting India's constitution is long and convoluted. Although the founding fathers of the United States took just 116 days to draft the U.S. Constitution, India's founders required nearly three years to see it finished. Three hundred members of the Constituent Assembly met to agree to its tenets, debating thousands of individual amendments to the document.

Although the Constitution of India draws most of its inspiration from British law, it also includes many other nations' tenants, including the American concept of a bill of rights and judicial review, the Canadian concept of residual powers of the federal government, and even a Soviet-inspired planning commission for economic growth. Many of the tenets of the constitution would sound familiar to Western ears: India gives its citizens the right to freedom of speech and expression; freedom of conscience and the right to practice religion; and the freedom to assemble peaceably.

Folk dancers dance and celebrate Republic Day—Indian's celebration of the signing of the constitution.

India's constitution is, by far, the longest in the world today for any national government, coming in at 145,000 words—around the average length of one of the books in the Harry Potter series. It features more than 400 separate articles and has been amended no fewer than 101 times, most recently in 2017. This vast depth reinforces the vast differences among the various ethnic, cultural, tribal, religious, and linguistic groups that all occupy India.

Independence and National Holiday

India's Independence Day lands on August 15, commemorating the national independence from the British Empire in 1947, on the day when Britain's own parliament voted to give India full **sovereignty**.

The story of India's independence is a long and complex one. Most outsiders are familiar with the basic narrative of Mohandas Gandhi (also known as Mahatma Gandhi; the term *Mahatma* is a Sanskrit honorific meaning "the great soul" and a person of high respect) and his nonviolent resistance to British rule. He is one of many revolutionary figures in modern Indian history, however, and not all of his contemporaries practiced nonviolence.

The first prime minister of India, Jawaharlal Nehru, signing the constitution.

Nations in the News: INDIA

A reveler takes part in the Independence Day celebration.

Indian independence can often be seen as a reflection of broader **nationalism** adopted throughout the late nineteenth and earlier twentieth century. Prominent Indian thinkers like Sri Aurobindo advocated for an independent Indian state well before Gandhi's rise to prominence; nineteenth-century Indian writers, artists, politicians, and intellectuals all contributed to an idea of a nation free from the harsh, exploitive, and racist policies of the British Empire. The British, who had become tremendously wealthy from the India colony by virtue of raw materials like cotton, silk, tea, and opium (as well as an exclusive market of hundreds of millions of people), arrested and even executed many revolutionaries. The Indian National Congress adopted Gandhi's nonviolent resistance in 1920. The national challenge to British authority steadily gained worldwide sympathy, but it would not be until the aftermath of World War II that the British Empire relinquished the colony that had once been called the jewel of its crown.

Other Indian national holidays include Republic Day on January 26, the day the constitution of India was adopted, and Gandhi Jayanti on October 2, the birthday of Mahatma Gandhi.

Discover more about Mahatma Gandhi.

Legal System

India boasts one of the longest histories of laws in all of human civilization. The first legal writings date as far back as 2,400 years ago, well before the earliest surviving laws of ancient Rome. This tradition is reflected in modern India, which surpassed the United States in 2011 to become the nation with the most lawyers.

India's constitution is held as the supreme law of the country, higher than its parliament or prime minister. Law created by the Union, the national government, supersedes that of state law. The Indian penal code is the highest criminal law in the country; like the constitution of India, it is also fairly long, weighing in at more than 500 separate sections.

Like so much else, Indian law reflects the country's cosmopolitan makeup. It has features of civil and common law, in addition to customary and religious laws in certain vicinities, one of the few holdovers of precolonial law.

Political Parties

The number of political parties throughout India reflects the vibrancy of the nation's democracy. There are seven nationally recognized political parties, meaning parties that have fulfilled the minimum requirements for obtaining enough votes to appear in the legislature. Listed alphabetically, they include the following:

1) All Indian Trinamool Congress

2) Bahujan Samaj Party

3) Bharatiya Janata Party

Leader of the All Indian Trinamool Congress, Mamata Banerjee.

4) Communist Party of India
5) Indian National Congress
6) Marxist Party of India
7) National Congress Party

This, however, applies only to the top of the political heap—an additional 1,800 parties are registered to appear in Indian elections. In a nation where poverty has bred illiteracy, many of these political parties are better known by their symbol, such as the coconut of the Goa Forward Party or the ladder of the Indian Union Muslim League.

The seven parties with the famous distinction of being nationally recognized are empowered to their own fair share of free broadcast time and allowed to participate in setting election dates and electoral guidelines. Some of these parties date back to the colonial era of politics, whereas others only recently arrived on the national scene.

Government and Politics

IN THE NEWS
The World's Biggest Voting Event

Hundreds of millions of Indians head to the polls for national elections, demonstrating that a single voice can matter in the largest nation on Earth. Some aspects of their elections may be familiar to outsiders, but others—including a "None of the Above" option on the ballot—reflect the complexity of the largest democracy in history.

The 2014 national election was the longest election in India's history and the largest election in the history of democracy itself. The Bharatiya Janata Party earned the most seats in the legislature, winning 282 out of 543 and thus securing a majority. It is a Hindu-nationalist political party, largely committed to economic growth and reform as well as the diplomatic and military prominence of India itself.

Executive Branch

There are two executive offices in India, that of the president and that of the prime minister, acting as the head of state and head of government, respectively. The constitution explicitly lays out the principle that the president will have executive power over the Union and the prime minister will be at the head of the Council of Ministers, who aid and advise the president. Each of these two executives has their own powers and prerogatives.

The prime minister can pick and choose any member to be part of the Council of Ministers as well as determine which highest-level posts in government go to which politicians. This makes the prime minister the de facto authority for a number of hugely important government agencies, ranging from India's space program to its nuclear research.

The prime minister must be a member of the legislature and, in theory, could hold the office indefinitely, so long as the president and/or legislature do not demand a new election or vote of confidence. Because prime ministers are also members of the legislature, they are expected to introduce and/or support various

Prime Minister Narendra Modi greets supporters after announcing his nomination in 2014.

pieces of legislation that are of the highest priority for their party. The longest-serving prime minister, Jawaharlal Nehru, served for 17 years. As of the 2014 election, India's prime minister is Narendra Modi. Interestingly, a 2010 survey by the *Economist* magazine discovered that India's prime minister is paid, by far, the least amount of money of any of the surveyed national executives: At the time, India's most important politician made just over $4,000 per year.

    The president must enforce the decrees of the legislature, defend the constitution as the commander in chief, and carry out changes enacted by the Supreme Court. The president is not elected directly by the people but instead by a vote of the legislature, serving for a term of five years. A vice president continues to carry out the president's responsibilities in the case of death, impeachment, resignation, or removal by the Supreme Court. The president can declare three

President Ram Nath Kovind.

specific types of emergencies: national, state, and financial; national emergency has only ever been declared during the 1962 war with China, the 1971 war with Pakistan, and in 1975–1977, when former prime minister Indira Gandhi claimed near-dictatorial powers. As of 2017, India's president is Ram Nath Kovind.

Legislative Branch

India's national legislature, the parliament, is divided into an upper and a lower house: the Rajya Sabha, or Council of States, 242 members strong, and the Lok Sabha, the House of the People, 545 members strong. As in many other mixed-parliamentary governments, the president of the nation has the authority to call both houses to create legislature. All legislative members of either house are called members of parliament (MPs).

Election to the House of the People is done through direct voting: Any Indian over the age of 18 who is not legally barred

In 2010, Barack Obama addressed the joint session of the parliament.

Women stand in line as they wait to cast their vote on election day.

Government and Politics 47

from voting is eligible to participate. These Indians vote on the national parties they wish to fill parliamentary seats, and the party that wins a plurality or majority of seats will have the most legislative power through that session. MPs in the House of the People have a term of five years. By contrast, individual state assemblies carry out elections for the Council of States, electing MPs to serve for six years with a number proportionate to their population size.

India's parliament conducts three separate sessions per year: the budget session, the monsoon session, and the winter session. By law, the president must summon a session at least every six months. A session will include not only work and debate on individual pieces of legislature but also parliamentary committees that research topics or propose solutions. Several standing parliamentary committees are devoted to enquiry, scrutiny, and passage of bills.

India's Supreme Court building is located in New Delhi.

Judicial Branch

India has a fiercely independent judiciary capable of interpreting law, rejecting policies, and solving disputes. Magistrates operate on a hierarchy with the nation's Supreme Court at the apex, above high courts, which hold hearings on issues specific to individual states. The Supreme Court is the final arbiter on all questions pertaining to the constitution. Unlike many other contemporary national courts, India's judiciary is independent to the point that legislators and executive officials cannot directly nominate members: The college of senior Supreme Court judges themselves recommends appointees for new seats. However, the president, with a majority of parliament, has the power to remove Supreme Court justices.

This degree of independence, along with the burden placed on it to interpret law, allows the Supreme Court to legislate from the bench to a far greater degree than many Western judiciaries. As an example, the Supreme Court had the authority in 2016 to declare that the country needed a new national disaster-relief agency, amalgamating many smaller, independent bodies. There are 24 high courts beneath the Supreme Court that also enjoy independence and the ability to interpret law.

A maximum of 30 justices sit on the Supreme Court of India as well as one chief justice, serving until the retirement age of 65; the chief justice is not appointed but instead is the senior-most member. Such a great size gives the court the ability to delegate cases and make more decisions. With over 24,000 resolutions since the foundation of the court in 1950, India's Supreme Court is one of the highest-volume courts around; by contrast, America's Supreme Court may hear only about 100 cases in a single year. Interestingly, both the Indian Supreme Court and the American Supreme Court hear their cases in the same language: English.

Size, however, has not created speed. India's courts are notoriously slow, with more than 20 million cases pending, about a quarter of which have been active for five or more years. Criticism of the judiciary includes the fact that thousands of appointments are still unfilled, sometimes including Supreme Court seats themselves. A report from 2014 indicated that two-thirds of all Indians currently in prisons had yet to be convicted of a crime.

Justice Ashok Bhushan is just one of the 27 Supreme Court justices in India.

Text-Dependent Questions

1. What is one foreign influence on the constitution of India?
2. When has India declared national emergencies in its history?
3. How often must the president of India call parliament?

Research Project

The constitution of India required a great deal of political maneuvering and compromise to be approved and ratified. Write a report about the founding fathers of India who contributed to the constitutional process. Who were some of the largest names, what were some of the most important political parties, and what were the most important concerns of the politicians who created the constitution?

CHAPTER 3

Economy

In 2006, India joined the international rankings as one of the emerging economic powerhouses of the twenty-first century, a grouping called BRIC: an acronym of Brazil, Russia, India, and China. (In 2010 South Africa entered the group, and it is now called BRICS.) Although corruption and recession have sent the economies of Brazil, Russia, and South Africa below tide level, India has risen to the challenge with scorching-hot growth. India's economy since

Words to Understand

Cash crop: Agriculture meant to be sold directly for profit rather than consumed.

Diaspora: Populations of people who no longer live in their homeland, spreading across the globe, sometimes retaining their culture and sometimes adopting new cultures.

Economic reserves: Currency, usually in the form of gold, used to support the paper money distributed through an economy, available to be used by a government when its own currency does not have enough value.

Nationalized: When an industry or sector of the economy is totally owned and operated by the government.

Trade deficit: The degree to which a country must buy more imports than it sells exports; can reflect economic problems as well as strong buying power.

As the economy grows, so does Mumbai's real estate market. Several skyscrapers have been constructed over recent years, adding to the city's skyline.

India's Economy at a Glance

Currency	Rupee; 2017 exchange rate: 65.17 rupees per U.S. dollar
Labor Force	521.9 million; 47 percent in agriculture, 22 percent in industry, 31 percent in services (2014)
Per Capita Income	$1,963 (2017)
Inflation Rate	3.6 percent (2017)
Gross Domestic Product (GDP)	$2.611 trillion (2017)
Overall Unemployment	8.8 percent (2017)
Industries	Textiles, chemicals, food processing, steel, transportation equipment, cement, mining, petroleum, machinery, software, pharmaceuticals
Imports	Crude oil, precious stones, machinery, chemicals, fertilizer, plastics, iron and steel
Import Partners	China 16.3 percent, United States 5.5 percent, United Arab Emirates 5.2 percent, Saudi Arabia 4.8 percent, Switzerland 4.7 percent (2017)
Exports	Petroleum products, precious stones, vehicles, machinery, iron and steel, chemicals, pharmaceutical products, cereals, apparel
Export Partners	United States 15.6 percent, United Arab Emirates 10.2 percent, Hong Kong 4.9 percent, China 4.3 percent (2017)

2012 has averaged six to eight percentage points of growth per year. India today is in the midst of its greatest economic boom in modern history. This, however, does not make it a system without flaws.

Currency and Banking System

The currency of India is the rupee, which is worth a little bit more than a cent. The name *rupee* is taken from an ancient Sanskrit word meaning a coin of silver, the oldest of which date back over 2,300 years. A dozen other Indian Ocean nations today also name their currency the rupee, a reflection of the popularity of these coins throughout the ancient Silk Road. The government issues banknotes with values between one and 2,000 rupees, all of which bear the iconic face of Mahatma Gandhi on their front. The rupee is commonly accepted throughout India's smaller neighbors like Bhutan and Nepal as well; interestingly, it is also legal tender in Zimbabwe due to the many trade connections between the two nations moving throughout the Indian Ocean.

Five mints produce India's national currency, and the Reserve Bank of India (RBI) determines monetary policy and maintains the

A shopkeeper counts rupees.

national **economic reserves** from its headquarters in Mumbai. With reserves worth about half a trillion dollars, India has the sixth-largest currency reserve in the world.

Though India's currency remains strong, especially throughout its local neighborhood, the mere mention of its banks gives many economists headaches. Officially, India's banking sector is modern, well regulated, and sufficiently capitalized by the Reserve Bank of India. Unofficially, state-owned Indian banks have swallowed up far too much bad debt owned by businesses (or former businesses), a reflection of overzealous investment pushes, bankruptcy laws that favor business owners, and plain old fraud. As more and more debt became pushed to the back of the books, looking uncertain if it would ever be repaid, India's national government stepped in during 2018 with a bailout package worth over $20 billion. Banks wrote off one in every six loans on their books. This came not a moment too soon: A study taken a few months after the bailout revealed that all 21 **nationalized** banks combined were worth less than the largest private bank, HDFC.

The Reserve Bank of India in Calcutta.

The economic success enjoyed by India is a striking contrast to the poor performance of many of the country's banks. It may suggest that many businesses in India's economy may be able to function even without steady access to credit, a rarity in the modern world.

Labor Force

India's staggering population of 1.3 billion means that any numbers about its workers are sure to dwarf those of every other nation except China. One of the least impressive numbers, however, is the overall labor force participation, currently ranked at 50 percent. This does not mean 50 percent of Indians are unemployed but rather demonstrates the great economic contrast in a nation that, while growing at record rates, still has tremendous levels of poverty. In total, about 500 million Indians contribute to the economy as workers, whether formal or informal.

Of the half not in the formal workforce, most find employment as farmers or laborers in rural areas. India's rural population stands at over 900 million; estimating information about such a workforce, let alone actually gathering data, presents a huge obstacle. This is complicated by the fact that 94 percent of the total working population are part of the unorganized sector (private business operations that are not officially registered by the government), lacking many of the formalities of a true business. These workers range from street vendors to fishermen to agricultural laborers.

The unorganized sector is recognized by its low wages, long hours, difficult labor, uncertainty, and poor productivity. Worse still, it is often characterized by debt bondage and child workers. Whereas the gross domestic product per capita of India stands at about $2,000 per year, the median (rather than average) per capita income is about half that figure, reflecting the depth of Indian poverty relative to the fast-growing wealth of parts of the population. Economists agree that India must transition the bulk of its labor force to the organized sector to compete with the wealthiest nations in the world.

India's ongoing industrial revolution has helped it to do so. Like other industrial revolutions (including that of North America), India's has created a major demographic shift of Indians who live and work in urban areas. Formal work with higher wages has drawn countless

Nations in the News:  INDIA

Unorganized labor, such as these street vendors, make up 94 percent of India's workforce.

Bazaars—or markets—are extremely popular in India. Street vendors sell a variety of goods, from clothing to food like popcorn, or flowers.

Nations in the News: **INDIA**

A man surveys coils of steel.

millions of people from the countryside to the cities. This has been a mixed blessing, where workers' earnings grow and their contributions to the economy are officially tallied, but uneducated workers may also live in slums with few, if any, modern comforts.

A Complex System

Every aspect of its mammoth labor force represents a challenge to the Indian government: how to count it, how to organize it, how to train it, and how to tax it. Labor law in India represents just as complex a challenge as other bureaucratic reforms due to the byzantine labor code that still includes colonial-era statutes. Criticisms of governmental labor practices include quasi-socialistic practices (the constitution of India refers to the nation as socialist, despite its thriving market economy) that attempt to encourage employment rather than efficiency; as an example, some companies must obtain permission from the government before firing an employee. A 2007 study revealed that India had the most restrictive labor laws of any country in the OECD (Organization for Economic Co-operation and Development, a group of nations more wealthy than average).

Poverty

Many topics that touch on India, including politics, geography, nature, and culture, emphasize the tremendous poverty of the country due to the fact that it impacts every facet of the country itself. India is not the poorest country in the world, but no other nation on Earth has more impoverished people by sheer volume. As of 2015, 736 million Indians live on less than two dollars in earnings per day. Despite the huge numbers, this reflects a tremendous success—the poverty rate dropped from 85 percent of the population in the early 1990s to just over half today.

Indian poverty has several key roots. British colonization sapped the country of natural resources and capital. India remains primarily an agricultural society in a country where space becomes more and more contested. A huge fraction of society—one person in four—cannot read, and perhaps half the population has no access to education. The issue of debt bondage affects as many as 20 million Indians, preventing them from ever climbing the social ladder.

A huge number of government initiatives try to keep poverty rates down. National campaigns to improve the lives of poor Indians

Women collect water from the local well. These families live in a slum.

Children sit among mounds of garbage in one of the poorest states in India—Raxaul.

Labor struggles in India.

through food subsidies, easy access to loans, medical care, sewage treatment, and family planning have all been praised for cutting down Indian poverty. Increased government support to farmers and food assistance programs to the poor have largely prevented famines, responsible in colonial times for creating death counts that rose into the millions.

Economy **61**

Agriculture

Organized agriculture as we know it has many of its roots in Indian civilization, when Neolithic tribes in the subcontinent some 10,000 years ago began to cultivate barley, wheat, cattle, and goats. Today, few nations are capable of producing more food by volume than India due to its tremendously fertile soil and the monsoon rains that drop huge quantities of water over much of the country.

Around 50 percent of the workforce contributes to agriculture in India, creating revenue equal to about 13 percent of national GDP. Although these numbers are declining due to rapid industrialization, they nevertheless fairly represent how important farming is to Indian society.

India is the world's leading producer of many fruits and vegetables, including bananas, lemons, mangoes, and chickpeas, in addition to spices like ginger and chili peppers. The huge number of cows in India and the importance of dairy in the vegetarian Hindu diet mean the country is also the world's leading producer of milk. Among staple crops, only China produces more wheat and rice by total volume than India. Like many other South and Southeastern Asian societies, rice represents the principal foodstuff for Indian peoples, and today the amount of rice grown per person in India

A shepherd tends to his herd of goats.

Fish farmers cast a net into the water.

exceeds the amount of rice consumed per person in Japan, a far wealthier nation. The fertile soils throughout India make it possible to grow many **cash crops**, most notably cotton and coffee, with a value typically much higher than normal food. Nonvegetarian populations of Muslims and Sikhs provide demand for meat, fish, and poultry. Although aquaculture is booming throughout the world, it has truly taken off in India, which has risen to become the world's second-leading provider of farmed fish.

India's tremendous fertility has boosted its export markets. Even as the share of agricultural workers in the broader economy declined between 2004 and 2014, Indian agricultural exports ballooned from $5 billion per year to nearly $40 billion per year—more than double the entire agricultural export value of the European Union, although it is still well behind China and the United States.

The long history of Indian crop failures and famines makes its agricultural planners look nervously toward harvest yields. Some evidence suggests that India's population is growing faster than its farmers can provide food for it; other evidence suggests that improvement to crop productivity, transportation, and food storage could not only feed India's next generation but also create an even

IN THE NEWS

How Technology Is Taking over Agriculture in India

The stereotypical view of most Indian farms is that of a premodern, primitive operation—a single family doing work by hand and, if they're lucky, a water buffalo to help with planting and harvesting. In reality, Indian agriculture depends more and more on technology with each day. Such new practices include the use of satellite imagery to collect massive amounts of data on a given area of land, helping government officials and farmers predict crop yields.

larger export market for food. This is far easier said than done, however, especially in regions of the country without access to education, electricity, or even motor vehicles.

Industries

Few nations have come out of the global economic depression of 2008 looking better than India. Its record economic growth, hitting highs of 7 to 8 percent with regularity, reflect the speed with which India has adopted many tenets of a modern economy, including manufacturing and industry.

Like all modern economies, Indian industries can broadly be divided into three key sectors: primary, secondary, and tertiary. The primary sector remains the largest by far, responsible for harvesting and refining raw materials ranging from coal to cotton. The secondary sector produces finished goods for direct consumption, and the tertiary (or service) sector helps businesses to perform at peak capacity. The growth of the service industry, now accounting for over half of all GDP, reflects India's newfound prominence among the other major economies of the globe.

Economic reforms in the 1990s that modernized foreign investment allowed many sectors to grow with an infusion of outside money. No industry benefited more than the textile industry, which is a monster. India boasts 2,500 textile-weaving factories and nearly twice as many textile-finishing factories. In total, the

Workers carry coal in baskets from the mines to a collecting spot where it will then be transferred and processed.

Indian textile industry accounts for 25 percent of all manufactured goods in India, provides direct employment for 45 million people, and produces about 15 percent of all textiles worldwide.

India has also benefited hugely from the rise of its information technology industry. A century of Indian **diasporas** that encouraged the smartest and most successful thinkers to work abroad has begun to reverse: More of India's homegrown intellectual talent enters its technology sector each year. As a result, India produces everything from microchips to computer hardware to server farms. IT has boomed throughout India, quadrupling its contribution to the national economy sixfold between 1998 and 2008, a reflection of its industries being able to compete on the global market. The city of Bangalore is often referred to as the "Silicon Valley" of India, whereas the city of Hyderabad is sometimes jokingly called "Cyberabad."

Commodities

India has modest reserves of fossil fuels and often must import the difference. Her greatest poverty relative to industrial needs is oil:

Although India has about one billion tons of crude oil reserves, annual production provides only about 20 percent of the market's demand. As a result, India is the fourth-largest importer of oil in the world and purchases most of its oil from Iraq and Iran. India is poised to grow its economy to the point that it may be a major power, but the lack of access to oil will be a major impediment: As of 2018, a gallon of gasoline costs about four dollars in India. The Indian oil industry is partially nationalized. Coal is far more plentiful in India, which has the fifth-largest reserves of coal in the world. However, much of India's coal is one of the dirtiest strains and directly contributes to the major air-quality issues in large Indian cities.

The ongoing global shift from fossil fuels to green energy will benefit India tremendously. Millions upon millions of farms make India a net exporter of virtually every agricultural product: It is a global leader in production of cotton, corn, wheat, rice, coffee, wool, milk, oilseeds, and sugar. Economic estimates about improvements to India's farmland and roads suggest that significant growth of

Oil rigs off the coast of Mumbai.

Nations in the News: **INDIA**

A farmer sorts through corn kernels.

agricultural output remains possible. Agro-waste itself is a valuable source of fuel in rural regions, suggesting a great deal of food, cloth, and oil is left in the fields each year.

India has small reserves of precious and non-precious metals. Supplying about 1 percent of the world's gold and much less of the world's silver, India imports far more precious metal than it digs from the ground, especially because the roaring economy has created a huge demand for luxury goods and jewelry. India has enough iron reserves to supply its economy, but laws meant to guarantee employment put national limits on iron mining and make it far more profitable for companies to import finished steel.

Imports and Exports

India's favorable geographic location, surrounded by an ocean that provides easy access to the global market, makes it a major importer of many raw and finished goods. India imports about

$75 billion more goods than it exports, giving it a **trade deficit**. The largest imports are petroleum, gold, and coal. India's growing smartphone market can reflect its broader trend of modernization: India imports $10 billion worth of telephones per year.

With an agrarian economy that employs half the population, India's exports are overwhelmingly agricultural: Rice, wheat, vegetables, garlic, sugarcane, coffee, seed oil, and lentils make up the most lucrative sales. India is one of the world's largest exporters of diamonds, selling $40 billion worth of precious stones overseas each year. Its car-export market has grown steadily and is now worth $6 billion. Both foreign and domestic car manufacturers in India assemble about 25 million vehicles per year.

Energy

Breakneck economic growth requires a huge amount of energy. India is now the world's third-largest consumer of energy, trailing only the United States and China, using 350 gigawatts of power per year. (For comparison, New York City burns up a gigawatt of power every two months.) This is much more energy than India itself can provide, meaning the country must import nearly half of its oil, gas, and coal.

Coal itself is the dominant source of electricity, providing about 56 percent of all energy, followed by petroleum at 29 percent, with small proportions of nuclear, hydro, and natural gas energy making up the remainder. Despite India's successful nuclear weapons program, India has just 22 nuclear power generators compared to 119 coal-fired power plants. In the wake of the 2011 Japanese Fukushima disaster, protests have slowed or stalled plans to build six new nuclear reactors.

India nationalized its coal industry in the 1970s and only in 2018 repealed the law to reprivatize its mines. Even so, the quality of Indian coal is not high and has directly led to tremendous air-quality issues in major cities: 11 of the 12 cities with the world's worst air pollution can be found in India (the other, Bamenda, is located in Cameroon). Medical studies indicate that the average Indian has only two-thirds the lung functionality of the average European.

Text-Dependent Questions

1. Why do economists criticize Indian labor laws that maximize employment?
2. What is the largest segment of India's economy after agriculture?
3. Why do smartphone imports reflect the larger Indian economy?

Research Project

India's membership in BRICS reflects very high expectations about economic growth. Research the BRICS organization and write an essay about your findings. What goals do its members have? What struggles will their economies have to overcome?

CHAPTER 4
Quality of Life

The contrast between the wealthiest and poorest parts of India is perhaps the most tremendously stark of any nation in the world. Wealthy, educated Indians have access to every amenity available to modern societies. An Indian farmer, by contrast, may live in a house of mud, draw water from wells, and rely on firewood for heat and light. In an economy where the average person makes about two dollars per day, the standards of living change drastically throughout India. Many promising signs indicate success, yet much more needs to be done.

Basic Human Needs

Every Indian city like Mumbai or Delhi has features familiar to the industrialized world: electrical grids, mass transit, water and sewer lines, and an abundance of places to purchase food. A village 100

Words to Understand

Disenfranchise: To take away someone's rights.

Dowry: Money given before a marriage by the bride or the bride's family to the groom and his family.

Infanticide: The intentional killing of infants.

Patriarchal: Society run by men, often taking away the rights or opportunities of women.

The slums of India are filled with difficult living conditions. Houses are made of mud and brick and often draped with tarps.

India's Quality of Life at a Glance

Life Expectancy at Birth	68.8 years
Maternal Mortality Rate	174 deaths/100,000 live births
Infant Mortality Rate	39.1 deaths/1,000 live births
Physician Density	0.76/1,000 population
Prevalence of HIV/AIDS in Adults	0.2 percent (2017)
Prevalence of Obesity in Adults	3.9 percent (2016)
Improved Sanitation Facility Access	Urban: 62.6 percent of population; rural: 28.5 percent of population; total: 39.6 percent of population
Improved Drinking Water Source	Urban: 97.1 percent of population; rural: 92.6 percent of population; total: 94.1 percent of population
Literacy	71.2 percent of population
Electricity Access	79 percent of population
Telecommunications Access	Fixed line: two subscriptions per 100 people; cellular: 91 subscriptions per 100 people
Internet Access	29.5 percent of population
Broadcast Media	Doordarshan, India's public TV network, has a monopoly on terrestrial broadcasting and operates about 20 national, regional, and local services; a large and increasing number of privately owned TV stations are distributed by cable and satellite service providers

Like most major big cities, the people of Mumbai have the opportunity to use public transportation. Buses and trains make it easier for people to get around.

miles away, by contrast, may have none of these. Although the divide between India's rich and poor is not strictly that of urban and rural, it may be easier to think of it this way to understand the contrast. India's growing economy has primarily benefited the urban centers and improved their quality of life by leaps and bounds; even so, poverty is typical, and often very visible, in Indian cities, too.

Nutrition and Basic Medical Care

India ranks 100th on the 119 nations listed in the Global Hunger Index. A large population in conjunction with high poverty makes it tremendously difficult to feed hundreds of millions of hungry mouths. One in four malnourished people worldwide lives in India, as does one in three stunted children worldwide. Although food production in India has doubled since 1998, the total number of Indians who do not get adequate nutrition may number as high as 200 million. Women and children are the most affected: Half of all women between the ages of 18 and 49 are anemic, whereas eight million infants living in India today were born weighing less than 5.5 pounds (2.5 kilograms).

Despite a constitutional guarantee of free health care and government hospitals that offer services free of cost, most Indian citizens live far away from the nearest doctor. There is just one doctor in India for every 2,000 people; the United States and Canada have five times as many doctors per person. Few Indian doctors work for the national health-care service itself—just one in five—and it is difficult to find volunteers willing to practice medicine in remote areas. Health-care providers and hospitals operate throughout India for those who can afford to pay, but few Indians can bear the cost of medical insurance, so most health-care costs must instead be paid out of pocket. Access to hospitals is not equal throughout India, furthermore, and instead depends on categories like income, gender, and place of residence.

In 2015 India failed to reach the health goals set out by the UN's Millennium Development Goals 15 years earlier. These goals included ending hunger, improving access to medicine, and reducing child mortality. India has signed on to the UN Sustainable Development Goals for 2030, however, which replaces the MDGs with new initiatives to reduce both hunger and poverty.

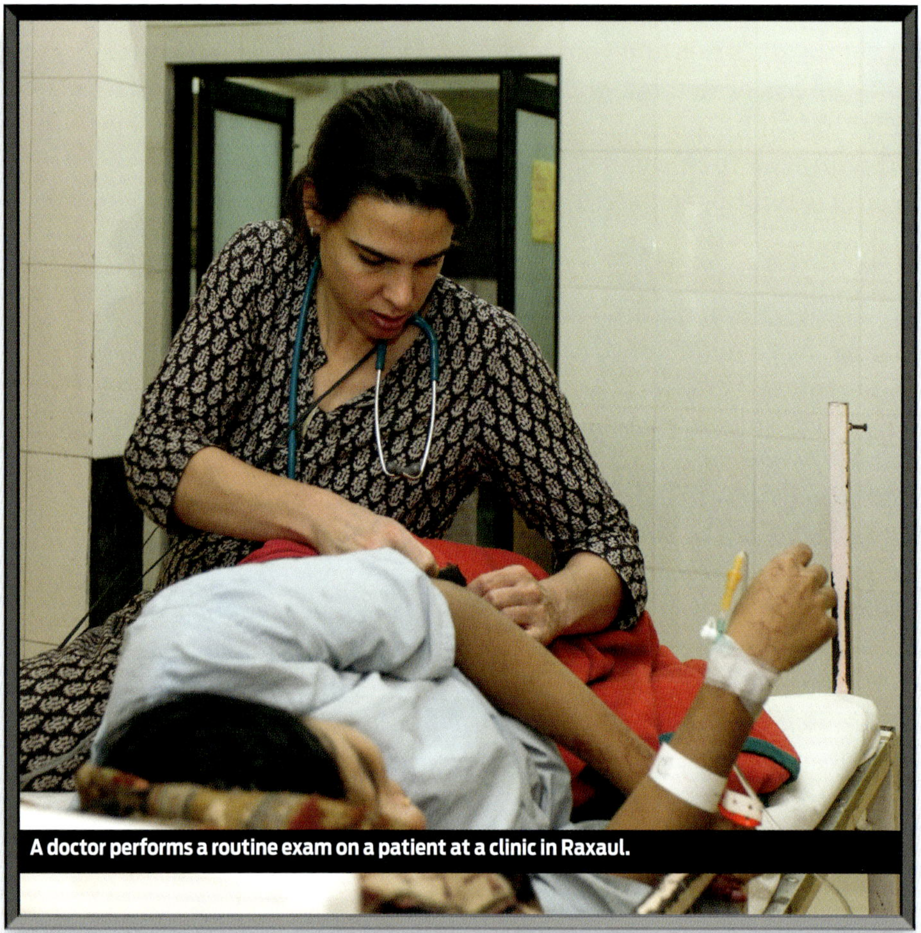

A doctor performs a routine exam on a patient at a clinic in Raxaul.

Water and Sanitation

Water is not hard to come by in many parts of India, with the exception of the western desert. Each year, monsoon clouds dump enough water on India to power the growth of farms and rain forests alike. A third of the population, 400 million people, live in the Ganges River Basin, where the fourth-largest river in the world provides enough water for India as well as Bangladesh. Despite the availability of water, not all Indians have access to clean water, and waterborne diseases remain problematic: 500 children under the age of five die of diarrhea each day.

About 90 percent of the Indian population has access to treated water, up from about 70 percent of the population in 1993. This, however, does not mean direct access—only one in four Indians has drinking water at home. For the other hundreds of millions, daily and even hourly trips to wells or springs or communal fountains are needed for cooking, cleaning, bathing, and drinking. The task of fetching water is one of many chores that is almost exclusively the responsibility of women: Just 15 percent of men in India fetch their own water. Two in three households draw, but do not treat, drinking water.

Poor water quality would be bad enough on its own, but India is famously unhygienic when it comes to sanitation. Twenty percent of the instances of all diseases in India are linked to poor water supply or poor sanitation. Half the population defecates in the open; just 7 percent do so in next-door Bangladesh. Half the population do not wash their hands with soap after defecation, while fewer than half wash their hands prior to preparing food or eating. Half of all mothers dispose of their children's feces in the open. Only 31 percent of the Indian population use plumbing and improved sanitation. As few as one in 20 rural Indian children uses toilets.

Women make trips to the local well to make sure they have drinkable water for their families.

Quality of Life

Sanitation and access to clean water remains one of the greatest challenges facing the Indian government today. Estimates suggest the financial cost of India's sanitation is well over $100 billion, an amount equal to about 5 percent of its gross national product. The Clean India Initiative has built over 50 million new toilets throughout the country but still must educate and motivate a huge part of the population to break from traditional practices for the sake of public health.

Shelter

A look at the Mumbai skyline at night makes it clear to visitors that India has entered the world of the twenty-first century. High-rises and skyscrapers compete for attention, climbing taller and taller, offering places to live and work for those who can afford it. Yet most of India cannot afford to live in anything except a home that they have built on their own out of mud bricks or sheets of scrap metal. Many houses in India grow larger as successive generations add new rooms by hand with simple materials.

A man collects trash near a dam on the Yamuna River.

Mumbai's skyline at night resembles many other major cities. It reflects the success it has had in the financial, commercial, and entertainment industries.

Housing in India, like so much else, reflects the great income inequality throughout the country. Huge blocks of low-rise apartment buildings provide shelter with running water and electricity for a city's workforce, while rural families may live in a one-room hut or shack.

One of the greatest challenges for housing in India is the huge slum population. Huge numbers of the urban poor—tens of millions—live in slum neighborhoods where factors like overcrowding, gang violence, and disease cut down the quality and duration of life significantly. The Dharavi slum of Mumbai is the largest slum in Asia, populated by one million people who live in metal shacks and have no access to running water. Dharavi, like many Indian slums, dates back over a century to the colonial era. Members of the *Dalit* caste, "the Undesirables," are the most common slum-dwellers, tasked with unclean professions like tanning or sewage disposal.

Personal Safety

How safe you are in India often depends on where you are. The state of Nagaland in the northeast has a crime rate lower than that of any U.S. state, whereas the state of Kerala in the southwest has

Life in the slums of India.

a crime rate 10 times higher. India's prison population is about 350,000, the fifth highest in the world, although its per capita imprisonment is lower than that of Switzerland.

India's culture has historically looked the other way about violence against women. Only in recent years have attacks on women become more widely reported, leading to ever-increasing numbers; an attack against an Indian woman occurs every three seconds. Modernization campaigns, both within the country and from outside, have struggled to reduce the impact of gender violence. Two out of three Indian men say that violence against women is acceptable for the purpose of keeping a family together and that women sometimes deserve to be beaten. The 2011 International Men and Gender Equality Survey revealed that one in four Indian men had committed sexual assault against a woman at least once in their lives.

There are many facets of violence against women. One prevalent issue is **dowry** murders. It is still typical throughout India for wives to have dowries, amounts of money given before a marriage by the bride or the bride's family to the groom and his family. Husbands and new in-laws will pressure, kidnap, beat, and even murder women in the hopes of increasing the dowry that she would bring in. The horrific practice of bride-burning, where a woman is either murdered or commits suicide by setting herself on fire, accounts for thousands of deaths per year. Other traditional aspects of Indian society, such as honor killings, continue to **disenfranchise** women: A woman who refuses to enter an arranged marriage, has had sex outside of wedlock, or has even been raped is thought to bring dishonor to a family and may be killed by her parents, siblings, or neighbors.

Women march against domestic violence.

Personal Well-Being

Many indices of well-being in India suggest that economic growth has brought good times. A 2011 study from the Cato Institute noted that metrics such as television ownership, cellphone ownership, and vehicle ownership had risen across the board in India, even among the lowest *Dalit* caste. Another interesting survey in 2017 from Mastercard indicates that India ranks very high for consumer optimism for overall well-being: The 2017 Well-Being Index rated Indian consumers as the most optimistic of any nation.

Education

Education is both free and compulsory for children between the ages of six and 14, established by the Constitution of India. Both public and private schools help to educate hundreds of millions of Indian children each day. Both have proven successful at raising India's literacy rates and helping to modernize its workforce; much of India's current economic success is attributed to successes in its classrooms. Efforts to educate more rural and impoverished children have resulted in 95 percent enrollment through the country, a total

Schoolchildren sit and listen to their teacher during a lesson in an outdoor classroom.

of over 200 million students. These efforts were both national and international: The World Bank has invested $2 billion in Indian education since 2000. Even so, India spends just 2.7 percent of its GDP on schools, lower than most other industrialized countries.

This means that although India has many success stories about education, it has many more stories of failures. Analyses of the education system from 2017 revealed that half of nine-year-old Indian schoolchildren cannot do simple mathematical sums, whereas half of those aged 10 cannot read a paragraph meant for seven-year-olds. The average Indian teenager would rank in the bottom 2 percent of an American class. Girls are far less likely than boys to complete school or even be able to read.

This contrast—growth in literacy but failure of more advanced learning—reflects the culture of education in India itself. Pupils advance to the next grade each year regardless of performance. Many teachers are not held accountable for their students' performances, because the same laws that make it difficult to fire workers keep teaching careers steady. About a quarter of all teachers do not make it to class on any given day, a reflection of teachers being given ample time off for personal and official reasons or for teacher training or administrative duties, or even difficulty commuting to schools themselves because some teachers must travel two hours a day to reach their school. Many teachers paid bribes to receive their position, looking at the role as an easy, do-nothing job where they have no fear of their paychecks coming in late. Teachers' unions shield their members against any and all grievances.

Many parents have chosen to look for outside help. For-profit schools have eagerly stepped in: There are now five private schools in India for every seven public schools. In 2008, India's private-education business was worth half a billion dollars, a figure that has since been projected to grow to over $40 billion.

Information Access

The growth of technology throughout India has put it front and center of the information economy. India today is the second-largest Internet market, behind only China, with about a quarter of the population able to access the Internet. Unlike China, furthermore, India does not restrict Internet access, even though it does not reach

A man browses through a large selection of books.

Indian newspapers sell 80 million copies daily.

far past the cities. Like many other parts of society, India's Internet use overwhelmingly favors men. Women account for only about a quarter of Internet activity.

India has a long history of journalism dating from the colonial era and today features 80 million daily newspaper sales—second only, yet again, to China. Unlike China, Indian newspapers are not chained to the government and instead are free to comment on politics, nationwide issues, and the national character. The Hindi-language *Dainik Jagran* is the nation's most-read newspaper, with a daily circulation of 3.6 million, making it the 17th-most-read newspaper in the world.

The growth of television in India well exceeds that of any other nation. Despite the nation's poverty, half of all households own a television and have access to nearly a thousand different channels. Indian soap operas dominate the airwaves, famously drawing in millions of viewers and stretching story lines out for years or even decades.

All India Radio, the public broadcast of the Indian government, is the largest radio network in the world, both in terms of total households reached and the spectrum of different languages (23 in total) for broadcasts. It reaches 99 percent of the population and until 1993 was the only radio broadcaster in the entire country.

Environment

It is not yet possible to modernize an economy without tremendous damage to an environment, and India is no exception. The environmental toll taken on the country in just the past century has been huge: Populations of species like the Indian rhinoceros, river dolphin, and snow leopard have been pushed to the brink of extinction. The Ganges may be the most polluted river in the entire world. The air quality in every major Indian city is so poor that it takes years off the lives of the inhabitants, a result of traffic congestion, coal-fired power plants, and the use of firewood as a primary fuel. The city of Kanpur has the highest small-particulate pollution level in the world, three times higher than the smog of Los Angeles.

Another major environmental concern is deforestation. India's rain forests were some of the largest in the world prior to colonization, when the population was less than a sixth of what it is today. Much of the Indian subcontinent has since been deforested to provide farmland and living space for the 1.3 billion people who call it home today. Commercial forestry has accelerated the loss of India's rain forests. In a population that largely depends on firewood for heating and light, India loses trees and produces atmospheric carbon at a rapid rate. Flooding in the wake of deforestation, furthermore, often results in soil erosion and destruction of habitat.

Habitat destruction has forced many wild animals to live in or around Indian cities. There are estimated to be 21 leopards living in the city of Mumbai. These predators ambush livestock or pets left out in the open and have even attacked and killed people, including a famous stretch in 2002 to 2004 when no fewer than 84 leopard attacks resulted in dozens of deaths. Other animals famously get along fine in cities: The famous rhesus macaques of Jaipur have become synonymous with the city itself, establishing troupes in each neighborhood and fighting over access to sites like temples, where generous human handouts provide all the food they need.

As a contrast to flooding, depleted water reserves represent a new risk to India's environment in drier areas. Although monsoons replenish the river each year during the rainy seasons, they do not reach every part of India. The western half of the country is desert and scrub, much less densely populated, yet human activity has steadily taxed the water resources of regions like Rajasthan, drying up rivers and emptying aquifers.

IN THE NEWS
Air Pollution in India

Air pollution in India is far worse than anywhere else in the world. Rapid industrialization has resulted in many environmental compromises, including a massive carbon footprint and extremely poor air quality. One recent medical study found that a quarter of all premature deaths in India in 2015 could have been linked to air pollution. Wealthy residents can afford to buy expensive imported air-purification systems, but for the majority of India's urban population, this is not an option. The problem of air pollution may soon develop into a national emergency.

Opportunity

Like so much else in Indian society, opportunities are widely available to the wealthy and middle class, whereas the poor may have few such opportunities. Even so, some indices indicate that social mobility in India is just as strong as it is in the United States. A 2016 study from the Global Development Institute found that urban opportunity vastly outpaced rural opportunity. About one-quarter of the urban Indian boys born to the lowest class of workers (such as construction laborers) managed to reach employment in the highest class of workers (such as government offices). By contrast, only about 10 percent of rural Indian boys born to the lowest classes of workers reached these heights. As in many other cases, caste defines opportunity: The *Dalit* caste have far fewer chances to climb the social and economic ladder.

 Nations in the News:

Tolerance and Inclusion

India is a famously intolerant society in many separate ways, but none more so than its caste system. Despite laws abolishing caste discrimination, this socioethnic hierarchy is entrenched in Indian society based on thousands of years of history. Classical Hindu texts like the *Mahabharata* commented on the importance of organizing society by caste in order to properly assign all people roles and work.

Caste hierarchies separate Indian society into explicit, immovable tiers: Those at the top are the priests and scholars, followed by warriors, then farmers and laborers, and finally the *Dalits*, the Undesirables, who perform jobs like clearing away sewage and are forced to live in filthy slums, with about half the national population living below the poverty line. It is no exaggeration to say that millions of Indians who are part of the *Dalit* caste have some of the worst living standards in the entire world. Progress has been made (including the election of India's first *Dalit* president, K. R. Narayanan, in 1992), but the caste system keeps India deeply unequal.

This, unfortunately, is not India's only major concern with equality. The status of women in India is notoriously poor. India ranks 127th out of 164 nations in gender equality. Although women enjoy constitutional rights like equality, dignity, and protection under the law, India's **patriarchal** society remains a more powerful cultural force than the law. Spousal abuse and marital rape represent serious issues that have historically gone unreported or underreported. Female **infanticide** in India is sadly prevalent because families choose to abort female fetuses or kill female infants in favor of males, who are expected to care for the family in its old age.

Homosexuality in India has not widely been accepted, although a 2018 court ruling legalized homosexual intercourse in a landmark case, throwing out a colonial-era law that referred to it as an "unnatural offense." Previously, a 10-year jail term could be given to those accused of this offense. Even so, gay couples cannot legally marry or obtain civil relationships. Prior to 2014, it was illegal for individuals to undergo sex-reassignment surgery, but today there are over four million transgender persons in India.

Higher Education

As in its primary education, India's higher education has been alternately praised for its achievements and blamed for its inefficiencies. India's higher education system is larger than any other nation's save those of the United States and China, and nearly 70 million Indians have a college education. In the state of Delhi, almost one-quarter of the population has a college degree, a higher ratio than the American states of West Virginia, Arkansas, and Mississippi. India has nearly 800 universities and 40,000 government degree colleges that provide licensing and training; both figures have increased tenfold since India's independence in 1947. Indira Gandhi National Open University is the largest institution of higher education in the world with 3.5 million students, located both in India and abroad. Like primary education, much of India's higher education is private.

India's higher education system is limited by the shortage of potential students, because just 7 percent of Indian students complete high school. With a gross enrollment ratio that is far worse than industrialized nations, India may produce millions of doctors

Students walk through campus at Banares Hindu University.

and engineers but leave millions more without a chance to get the education needed for such a profession. For many colleges, this is a solution rather than a problem, because they cannot meet the minimum requirement standards for the students they do have in the first place.

Each problem in higher education is exacerbated by many more: More than half of Indian instructors at universities lack an advanced degree; enrollment by women has grown from 39 percent to 46 percent, but only about half continue from undergraduate to professional courses; some universities are wholly owned by the wealthy and use the student bodies for political purposes; and not even a quarter of Indian universities are accredited.

Despite the myriad of issues facing Indian universities, they still produce millions of new graduates each year, infusing new ideas and brainpower into an economy that desperately needs both. Although these universities have helped boost the economic boom, they must undergo major change to keep standards high and produce more of the specialists needed by an advanced economy.

Text-Dependent Questions

1. Why are most health-care costs in India paid out of pocket?
2. What is the major difference between access to the Internet in India compared to China?
3. Why do leopards live in Mumbai, a city of some 20 million people?

Research Project

To an outsider, the caste system of India seems a hugely unfair and restrictive social practice, yet many Indians consider it necessary or even crucial to their everyday life. Research the different tiers of the caste system. What are the responsibilities of each caste? Are there any similarities between India's caste system and the social or ethnic hierarchies that you and your friends occupy?

Chapter 5
Society and Culture

India has the second largest population in the world, but it is by far the most diverse. With 415 living languages on record spoken by dozens of different ethnic and tribal groups, there is no such thing (nor could there be) as a uniform Indian culture. However, the Hindi culture dominates much of India, even though hundreds of millions of Indians cannot speak or read Hindi.

Population

At 1.32 billion people strong, it can be hard to grasp the sheer size of India's population. It accounts for one-fifth of global population located in just one-fiftieth the world's landmass. You could cut it in half and still have a larger population than all of North America. India's population density in major cities like Mumbai reaches concentrations as high as 30,000 people per square kilometer. The census counts 680,000 individual villages. The country has a population larger than any continent besides Asia itself. And yet

Words to Understand

Demographic dividend: A society with few elderly people and many young people, meaning a large availability of workers with few social obligations.

Indigenous: A person or group native to a particular place.

Redress: To correct a negative situation.

Revelers dance and celebrate in the streets during Holi.

India's Society and Culture at a Glance

Population	1,281,935,911 (July 2017 est.)
Population Rank	2
Sex Ratio	1.08 males/females
Age Distribution	27.34 percent age 0–14; 17.9 percent age 15–24; 41.08 percent age 25–54; 7.45 percent age 55–64; 6.24 percent age 65 and over
Ethnic Groups	Indo-Aryan 72 percent, Dravidian 25 percent, Mongoloid and other 3 percent
Religions	Hindu 79.8 percent, Muslim 14.2 percent, Christian 2.3 percent, Sikh 1.7 percent, other and unspecified 2 percent (2017 est.)
Languages	Hindi 43.6 percent, Bengali 8 percent, Marathi 6.9 percent, Telugu 6.7 percent, Tamil 5.7 percent, Gujarati 4.6 percent, Urdu 4.2 percent, Kannada 3.6 percent, Odia 3.1 percent, Malayalam 2.9 percent, Punjabi 2.7 percent, Assamese 1.3 percent, Maithili 1.1 percent, other 5.6 percent

A crowded train station in Mumbai.

India's booming population.

India is still in second place to China—at least until 2024, when it is projected to overtake the world leader.

Age Distribution

India has often been called a **demographic dividend**, owing to its young population. High birth rates in India skew the population young: 10 percent are under the age of five, 40 percent under the age of 18, and just 6 percent above the age of 65. The average woman gives birth for the first time at the age of 20, even though the birthrate has dropped precipitously from six births per woman in 1964 to just 2.4 births per woman today. The life expectancy in India is 68 years, with women living slightly longer than men.

Nations in the News: INDIA

A mother holds her newborn child.

Sex Ratio

India's patriarchal society and social preference for male offspring is clearly reflected in its national sex ratio. There are 3.2 million fewer women in India than men, a result of a culture where men are expected to carry the family's burdens, whereas women are expected to serve their husband's family. The great desire for a son, and the fear of paying a huge sum of money for a daughter's dowry, lead to female infanticide and sex-selective abortions throughout India. This is yet another similarity India has with China, which also has a population tilted toward men.

The extreme difficulty in reporting and collecting information about India's infanticide makes it hard to generate conclusions. What's more, the process is not singular to any one demographic: The sex ratio of every major religious group in India reveals fewer female children than male children across each culture.

IN THE NEWS
India's Gender Imbalance

The government of India has made many attempts to **redress** the problem of gender imbalance and the tragedy of infanticide. Initiatives that made it possible to put girls up for adoption were hailed for having cut down on the number of infanticides. India's social mobilization campaign *Beti Bachao, Beti Padhao* ("save girl child, educate girl child"), launched in 2015, works to highlight the value of daughters and their potential to be family leaders and providers when given a good education.

Religions

With a secular constitution that guarantees the right to religion of choice for all, no nation on Earth balances every global religion like India does. Home to most of the world's Hindu population, most of the world's Sikh population, more Muslims than any nation except Indonesia and Pakistan, and millions more Christians and Buddhists to boot, India features sizable populations of every major religion. In India the god Vishnu caused all living things to rise up; the Buddha found enlightenment; and the Sikh prophet Guru Nanak spread the word of a new god.

Constitutional protection does not mean that all these religions live together in harmony, however. India rates as the fourth-worst nation in the world for religious violence, behind only Syria, Nigeria, and Iraq—all places with active war zones. India's past is littered with religious conflicts, especially between Hinduism and Islam—Hindus abhor that Muslims eat cows, and Muslims abhor the Hindu practice of praying before idols. In 2015, a crowd of Hindus lynched a Muslim man for eating beef. The divide of Kashmir itself reflects the larger Hindu-Muslim schism throughout Southern Asia, present from the start but exacerbated by colonial map divisions. Even so, violence between other religious groups, including Sikhs, Christians, and even atheists, has occurred throughout India.

The official Hindu population stands at just shy of a billion people, making them the clear majority of the population. Hinduism is the

A priest prays to the Goddess Durga during the Durga Puja festival.

oldest continually practiced religion in the world, dating as far back as 4,000 years into the Iron Age. Unlike many other global religions, Hinduism has no one founder or prophet but instead is a synthesis of religious texts, the Vedic literature, which were written thousands of years ago and believed to be the direct voice of the divine.

Islam is the next-most-practiced religion in India, accounting for about 190 million persons. Islam first came to India about 1,400 years ago but stuck mainly to the coastal communities; not until the Islamic Ghurid Empire conquered Delhi did it become a state religion and begin to spread past the largest cities. Broadly speaking, Muslims in India today are poorer and less educated than the majority Hindu population and have a higher birthrate; however, they are also more urban and have a lower infant mortality rate.

Christianity is the third-largest religion in India with 30 million followers, a direct legacy of British colonization. Christianity in India predates the British Empire by hundreds of years, however, because it was first brought to Indian shores by Thomas the Apostle ("Doubting Thomas") in the year 52. While just 2.5 percent of the population is Christian, three Indian states actually have majority Christian populations: the state of Mizoram is over 90 percent Christian.

Worshippers gather at the Taj Mahal for Eid al-Fitr.

Churchgoers attend a Catholic service at St. Patrick's Church in Bangalore.

Sikhism is the fourth major religion, beginning in India about 600 years ago when Guru Nanek began preaching and writing Sikh philosophy. Sikhism became popular in the Punjab region of the northwest despite the efforts of Islamic leaders to stamp out its spread. The Sikh Empire ruled this area from 1799 to 1849, representing the greatest spread of political Sikhism. Today 20

Nations in the News:  INDIA

Sikh men and women gather at the Golden Temple to light candles.

million Sikhs live in India, with a larger diaspora throughout the English-speaking world.

Ethnic Groups

The National Census of India does not provide specific recognition for multiple ethnicities, which is why all 1.3 billion Indians occupy one of just three major groups: Indo-Aryan (75 percent), Dravidian (20 percent), and other (5 percent). Nevertheless, the government does count the list of "scheduled tribes" and lists 700, whereas cultural anthropologists have identified some 2,000 separate ethnic groups.

The Indo-Aryan ethnicity broadly inhabits the northern regions of India, while also making up the majority of the population of Pakistan and Bangladesh. The Dravidians largely inhabit the southern half of the country. It is believed the Indo-Aryan ethnic group came to India about 4,000 years ago in a mass migration from Central Asia, whereas Dravidians appear likely to be the largest **indigenous** group of India.

Languages

Twenty-two nationally recognized languages and hundreds of unofficial languages make India the most linguistically diverse nation in the world. Even so, the Constitution of India lays out

A student reviews his letters during an English lesson.

only two official languages for government functions: Hindi and English. About one in four Indians is a native Hindi speaker, and another one in four speaks it as a second or third language; television and Indian cinema ("Bollywood") are broadcast primarily in Hindi. Simplified versions of Hindi, called pidgin languages, include Haflong Hindi and serve as a common language capable of being understood by more people throughout the country. Interestingly, Hindi is one of the youngest Indian languages by far, having only been standardized within the past 300 years.

India's English-speaking population numbers about 10 percent, making it the second-largest English-speaking nation in the world after the United States. Yet another legacy of British colonialism, Indian English is a unique dialect with little difference in pronunciation between the letters V and W or the letters S and Z. This is due to the fact that some of these letters do not appear in Indian languages at all, much like letters with accents do not appear in the English language.

Nations in the News:  INDIA

Foods

Perhaps the greatest cultural legacy of India is its food. Famous for basmati rice, naan bread, and tremendous varieties of spice, Indian food comes in as many styles as it has people. Hindu and Jain populations all practice vegetarianism, with staple foods of lentils and beans for sustenance. Without a doubt the most popular Indian food is curry, sauce dishes made from coriander, cumin, and turmeric, mixed with dairy or coconut milk. The term *curry* itself refers to curry leaves, which provide flavoring but are not the main ingredient in the food itself.

A broad north/south divide can be reflected in Indian food, where rice provides the bulk of the calories in the south and wheat (typically bread) provides the bulk of the calories in the north. Cheese, called *paneer*, adds valuable protein to vegetarian diets. Major cities on the coasts, most notably Goa, are famous for seafood meals and delicacies. A *sadha* is an entire feast delivered on a banana leaf, featuring a cluster of rice and two dozen accompaniments. *Pav bhaji* is India's answer to fast food, a thick vegetable curry served with a bread roll.

National Holidays

Individual states and even villages may have their own unique holidays and festivals separate from the three major national

A vendor prepares naan for hungry customers.

holidays. None are more famous than Holi, the Hindu Festival of Colors, celebrating the end of winter and the cosmic victory of good over evil. Diwali, the Hindu festival of lights, is observed throughout most of the country, symbolizing the spread of knowledge and peace. Every Indian state observes the major Muslim holidays of Ramadan, the month of fasting, and Mawlid, the birthday of the prophet Muhammad. The Sikh holiday of Vaisakhi celebrates the new year and the harvest.

Lentils are a staple food in India. Pictured here, vendors sell a variety of lentils at a street market.

Holi is celebrated with colorful powder and water.

During Diwali, it is common to see vendors selling marigolds. This flower represents new beginnings.

Text-Dependent Questions

1. Why does India have a demographic dividend?
2. What is the second most practiced religion in India?
3. Which major religious groups do not eat meat?

Research Project

The world's leading producer of movies is India. Its "Bollywood" industry churns out hundreds of movies per year. Look up information about Bollywood: What are similarities and differences between its movies and some of your favorite movies? What is unique about Bollywood in comparison to American filmmaking?

Society and Culture

Series Glossary of Key Terms

Absolute monarchy: A form of government led by a single individual, usually called a king or a queen, who has control over all aspects of government and whose authority cannot be challenged.

Amendment: A change to a nation's constitution or political process, sometimes major and sometimes minor.

Arable: Describing land that is capable of being used for agriculture.

Asylum: When a nation grants protection to a refugee or immigrant who has been persecuted in his or her own country.

Austerity: Governmental policies that include spending cuts, tax increases, or a combination of the two, with the aim of reducing budget deficits.

Authoritarianism: Governmental structure in which all citizens must follow the commands of the reigning authority, with few or no rights of their own.

Autocracy: Ruling regime in which the leader has absolute power.

Bicameral: A legislative body structured into two branches or chambers.

Bilateral: Something that involves two nations or parties.

Bloc: A group of countries or parties with similar aims and purposes.

Cash crop: Agriculture meant to be sold directly for profit rather than consumed.

Central bank: A government-authorized bank whose purpose is to provide money to retail, commercial, investment, and other banks.

Cleric: A general term for a religious leader such as a priest or imam.

Coalition force: A force made up of military elements from nations that have created a temporary alliance for a specific purpose.

Colonization: The process of occupying land and controlling a native population.

Commodities: Raw products of agriculture or mining, such as corn or precious metals, that can be bought and sold on the market.

Communism: An economic and political system where all property is held in common; a form of government in which a one-party state controls the means of production and distribution of resources.

Conscription: Compulsory enlistment into state service, usually the military.

Constituency: A body of voters in a specific area who elect a representative to a legislative body.

Constitution: A written document or unwritten set of traditions that outline the powers, responsibilities, and limitations of a government.

Coup: A quick change in government leadership without a legal basis, most often by violent means.

De-escalation: Reduction or elimination of armed hostilities in a war zone, often directed by a cease-fire or truce.

Defector: A citizen who flees his or her country, often out of fear of oppression or punishment, to start a life in another country.

Demilitarized zone: An area where military personnel, installations, and related activities are prohibited.

Depose: The act of removing a head of government through force, intimidation, and/or manipulation.

Détente: An easing of hostility or strained relations, particularly between countries.

Developing nation: A nation that does not have the social or physical infrastructure necessary to provide a modern standard of living to its middle- and working-class population.

Diaspora: The members of a community that spread out into the wider world, sometimes assimilating to new cultures and sometimes retaining most or all of their original culture.

Diktat: An order from an authority given without popular approval.

Disenfranchise: To take away someone's rights.

Displaced persons: Persons who are forced to leave their home country or a region of their country due to war, persecution, or natural disasters.

Economic boom: A period of rapid economic and financial growth, resulting in greater wealth and more purchasing power.

Economic reserves: Currency, usually in the form of gold, used to support the paper money distributed through an economy, available to be used by a government when its own currency does not have enough value.

Edict: A proclamation by a person in authority that functions the same as a law.

Embargo: An official ban on trade.

Federation: A country formed by separate states with a central government that manages national and international affairs, but control over local matters is retained by individual states.

Food insecurity: Being without reliable access to nutritious food at an affordable price and in sufficient quantity.

Free-floating currency: A currency whose value is determined by the free market, changing according to supply and demand for that currency.

Fundamentalist: A political and/or religious ideology based explicitly on traditional orthodox concepts, with rejection of modern values.

Gross Domestic Product (GDP): The total value of goods and services a country produces in a given time frame.

Hegemony: Dominance of one nation over others.

Heretical: When someone's beliefs contradict an orthodox religion.

Indigenous: Referring to a person or group native to a particular place.

Industrialization: The transition from an agricultural economy to a manufacturing economy.

Inflation: A general increase in prices and a decrease in the purchasing value of money.

Insurgency: An organized movement aimed at overthrowing or destroying a government.

Islamist: A military or political organization that believes in the fundamentals of Islam as the guiding principle, rather than secular law; often used synonymously (although not always accurately) with Islamic terrorism.

Jihad: A struggle or exertion on behalf of Islam, sometimes through armed conflict.

Judiciary: A network of courts within a society and their relationship to each other.

Mercantilism: A historical economic theory that focuses on the trade of raw materials from a colony to the mother country, and of manufactured goods from the mother country to the colony, for the profit of the mother country.

Migrant: A person who moves from place to place, either by choice or due to warfare or other economic, political, or environmental crises.

Militia: A group of volunteer soldiers who do not fight with a military full-time.

Municipal elections: Elections held for office on the local level, such as town, city, or county.

Nationalize: When an industry or sector of the economy is totally owned and operated by the government.

Parliamentary: Governmental structure in which executive power is awarded to a cabinet of legislative body members, rather than elected by the people directly.

Paramilitary: Semimilitarized force, trained in tactics and organized by rank, but not officially part of a nation's formal military.

Patriarchy: A system of society or government in which power is held by men.

Police state: Nation in which the state closely monitors activity and harshly punishes any citizen thought to be critical of society or the government.

Populism: An approach to politics, often with authoritarian elements, that emphasizes the role of ordinary people in a society's government over that of an elite class.

Propagandist: A person who disseminates government-created communications, like TV shows and posters, that seek to directly influence and control a national audience to serve the needs of the government, sometimes employing outright falsehoods.

Proportional representation: An electoral system in which political parties gain seats in proportion to the number of votes cast for those seats.

Protectionist: Actions on behalf of a government to stem international trade in favor of helping domestic businesses and producers.

Reactionary: A person who opposes new social and economic ideas or reforms; a person who seeks a return to past forms of governance.

Referendum: A decision on a particular issue put up to a popular vote.

Refugee: A person who leaves his or her home nation, by force or by choice, to flee from war or oppression.

Reparations: Payments made to someone to make amends for wrongdoing.

Republicanism: A political philosophy of representative government in which citizens elect leaders to govern.

Rubber-stamp legislature: Legislative body with formal authority but little, if any, decision-making power and subordinate to another branch of government or political party leadership.

Sanctions: Political and/or economic punishments levied against another nation as punishment for wrongdoing.

Secretariat: A permanent administrative office or department, usually in government, and the staff of that office or department.

Sect: A subgroup of a major religion, with individual beliefs or philosophies that divide it from other subgroups of the religion.

Sovereignty: The ability of a country to rule itself.

Statute: A law created and passed by a legislative body.

Subsidies: Amounts of money that a government gives to a particular industry to help manage prices or promote social or economic policies.

Tariff: A tax or fee placed on imported or exported products.

Theocratic: Of or relating to a theocracy, a form of government that lays claim to God as the source and justification of its authority.

Totalitarian: A form of government where power is in the hands of a single person or group.

Trade deficit: The degree to which a country must buy more imports than it sells exports; can reflect economic problems as well as strong buying power.

Trade surplus: The degree to which a country can sell more exports than it purchases; can reflect economic strength as well as poor buying power.

Welfare state: A system where the government publically funds programs to ensure the health and well-being of its citizens.

Chronology of Key Events

3300 BCE	Earliest evidence of Indian civilization, capable of writing, metalworking, irrigation, and boatbuilding.
1500 BCE	Beginning of Vedic period and production of the holy Hindu texts (*Vedas*).
563 BCE	Birth of Siddhartha Gautama, the first Buddha.
273 BCE	Ashoka the Great, widely remembered as India's greatest ancient ruler, becomes Mauryan Emperor.
100	Sugar first refined from sugarcane in India.
712	First Muslim conquests in India.
788	Birth of Adi Shankara, theologian credited with the Hindu doctrine of Advaita Vedanta, which continues to organize and guide Hindu thought.
1221	Genghis Khan invades northern India.
1498	Vasco da Gama's first voyage to India from Europe; European powers seize port cities like Goa to serve as trade centers.
1600	England's East India Company gets exclusive trade rights with India.
1858	Britain takes total control of India, creating the British Raj.
1947	India gains independence and immediately fights border war with Pakistan.
1948	Mahatma Gandhi assassinated.
1950	Constitution of India is ratified, and the Republic of India is formed.
1962	Border war with China.
1974	India successfully tests nuclear bomb.
1984	Prime Minister Indira Gandhi (unrelated to Mahatma Gandhi) assassinated.
1990	Muslim separatist groups in Kashmir begin insurgency.
1994	Pakistan successfully tests nuclear bomb.
2001	India launches rocket into space, beginning the Indian space program.

2002   Conflict in Kashmir and nuclear tests between India and Pakistan come close to the point of war.

2004   India applies to the United Nations for a permanent seat on the Security Council.

2010   Economic growth hits 10 percent.

2014   Narendra Modi becomes prime minster after his Bharatiya Janata Party wins overwhelming victory in the largest election in the history of democracy.

Further Reading & Internet Resources

Books

Boo, Katherine. *Behind the Beautiful Forevers: Life, Death, and Hope in a Mumbai Undercity.* New York: Random House, 2014. This intimate portrayal of slum life among the Mumbai poor offers a sobering contrast to the stories of India's growth and success, indicating how much work must still be done.

French, Patrick. *India: A Portrait.* New York: Vintage, 2012. This massive book, over 400 pages long, gives an exhaustive look at India's politics, economics, and place in the modern world.

Gandhi, Mohandas. *An Autobiography.* Boston, MA: Beacon Press, 1993. By far the most famous Indian in modern history and the father of the nation, Gandhi's experience and philosophy can be read in his own words by any student.

Kapur, Akash. *India Becoming: A Portrait of Life in Modern India.* New York: Riverhead Books, 2013. Kapur, a Rhodes Scholar and former journalist for the *International Herald Tribune*, lays out an intimate look at development through a number of anecdotes and personal experiences, indicating how some Indians are rising to the top while others are being left behind.

Rai, Vinay. *Think India.* New York: Plume Publishing, 2008. An examination of the factors that led to India's meteoric rise, ranging from its pharmaceutical industry to its research and development. The book provides a purposeful contrast to the American superpower to demonstrate the differences and similarities between the United States and India.

Roy, Arundhati, and Pankaj Mishra. *Kashmir: The Case for Freedom.* New York: Verso, 2011. A peaceful solution to the Kashmir problem between India and Pakistan appears all but impossible. Perhaps the only solution is for both to give it up and allow Kashmir to be its own sovereign nation.

Web Sites

Business Standard. http://www.business-standard.com. Reporting from the heart of India's economic boom, *Business Standard* includes coverage of markets, companies, finance, and politics.

India Today. http://www.indiatoday.intoday.in. A comprehensive news site, *India Today* has popular coverage of all topics, including government votes, weather forecasts, and scores of national cricket tests.

Northlines. http://www.thenorthlines.com. Independent news source relating to Kashmir and Jammu, established in 1995 to serve the far northern regions' readers.

Outlook India. http://www.outlookindia.com. A weekly English-language magazine published throughout the country, *Outlook India* is famous not only for its reporting but its beautiful photography.

Rising Kashmir. http://www.risingkashmir.com. The largest website devoted to news about the Kashmir province, *Rising Kashmir* not only analyzes political and military news but also the rarely reported culture and sports of Kashmir itself.

Scroll.in. http://www.scroll.in. Calling itself an independent news venture, *Scroll.in* focuses on lesser-heard stories and provides unique analysis on contemporary India.

The Asian Age. http://www.asianage.com. Launched in 1994, the *Asian Age* is India's first global newspaper with an emphasis on international topics, printed in Dehli, Mumbai, and London.

TechGenYZ. http://www.techgenyz.com. This site provides coverage of Indian startups, tech firms, and digital innovation.

Times of India. http://www.timesofindia.indiatimes.com. By far the largest and most well-trusted news site in India, the *Times of India* reports on everything from financial markets to film reviews.

Index

A
abuse, 14, 77–78
Afghanistan, 29, 32
age distribution, 89–90
agriculture, 6, 9–11, 62–64, 66–68
  See also cash crops
All India Radio, 83
alliances, 7, 14, 26–27, 34
  See also foreign relations
al-Qaeda, 21, 28–29, 34
Asian Development Bank, 26
Assamese (language), 89
atheism, 92
Aurobindo, Sri, 41

B
Baha'ism, 6
Banares Hindu University, 86
Banerjee, Mamata, 43
Bangalore, 65, 94
Bangladesh, 12, 24, 74–75, 95
banking, 54–55
Bengali (language), 89
Beti Bachao, Beti Padhao, 92
Bhushan, Ashok, 50
Bhutan, 28, 54
Bhutto, Zulfikar Ali, 26
Bollywood, 96, 99
Brazil, 29–30, 52
  See also BRICS
BRICS, 52, 69
bride-burning, 78
British Empire, 7, 11–12, 14, 20, 22, 36, 40–41, 93
British Raj, 11–12
Buddha, 92, 105

C
Calcutta, 15, 32
cash crops, 52, 62–63, 100
  See also agriculture
caste system
  current status of, 85
  definition of, 7
  and human trafficking, 31
  in the news, 19
  problem of, 14–15, 19
  structure of, 85
  See also Dalit
children, 31–32, 56, 61, 73–74, 80–81
China, 8, 11, 15, 22, 24–26, 28–30, 34, 52, 68, 81–82
  See also BRICS
Christianity, 89, 92–93
Clean India Initiative, 76
climate, 6, 8–10, 62
coal, 6, 12, 15, 65–66, 68, 83
colleges, 86–87
colonialism, 14–15, 22, 25, 41, 59–60, 77, 93, 96, 100
Commonwealth of Nations, 36, 38
conflicts, 14, 20, 22–31, 46, 92
Constituent Assembly, 39
Council of Ministers, 44
Council of States, 46, 48
counterterrorism, 28–29, 34–35
criminality, 32, 77–78
culture, 14, 19, 31–32, 78, 88, 91–99
currency, 52–55

D
Dainik Jagran, 82
Dalai Lama, 25
Dalit, 31, 77, 79, 84
debt bondage, 7, 14, 31, 56, 60
Delhi, 15, 19, 70, 86, 93
democracy, 36–44
demographics, 8–9, 15, 42, 56, 59, 63–64, 74, 88–92
diaspora, 52, 65
diet, 62–63, 97–98
diplomacy, 26–28
diseases, 71, 74–76
diversity, 14, 42, 88
Diwali, 98–99
Doordarshan, 71
dowries, 70, 78, 91
Dravidians, 89, 95
Durga Puja, 93

E
East Pakistan. *See* Bangladesh
economy, 12, 16, 25, 28–30, 33–34, 52–73, 79
  See also BRICS; trade
education, 13–14, 59–60, 64, 71, 75, 79–81, 86–87, 93
Eid al-Fitr, 94
elections, 36–39, 42–48
electricity, 64, 68, 71
energy, 19, 68
English (language), 49, 96
environment, 83
ethnic groups, 14–15, 88–89, 95
European Union (EU), 26, 28–29
executive branch, 36–38, 44–45
exploitation, 30–31, 56, 78
  See also abuse; children; women
exports, 11, 52–53, 63–64, 66–68
extinction, 83

F
fauna, 15, 20, 83
fertility rate, 63–64, 90
Festival of Colors, 98
Festival of Lights, 98
festivals. *See* holidays
foods, 62–63, 68, 97–98
foreign relations, 22–34
forests, 13, 15, 83
fossil fuels, 65–66, 68

G
Gandhi, Indira, 46, 105
Gandhi, Mohandas Karamchand, 20, 22, 40–42, 54
Gandhi Jayanti, 41
Ganges River, 8–9, 15, 74, 83
gender imbalance, 32, 90–92
geography, 6–11, 14, 25, 76, 88
Ghurid Empire, 93

Nations in the News:  INDIA

Global Development Institute, 84
Global Hunger Index, 73
gold, 13, 52, 67–68
Google Maps, 24
government, 36–51
green energy, 66, 68
gross domestic product (GDP), 20–21, 33, 56, 62, 64, 102
Group of Twenty (G20), 26
Gujarati (language), 89
Guru Nanak, 92, 94

H

Haflong Hindi (language), 96
health care, 61, 71, 73
Himalaya Mountains, 1, 7–8, 10
Hindi (language), 82, 88–89, 96
Hinduism, 7, 14, 22–24, 62, 85, 89, 92–93, 97–98, 105
history, 11–12, 22–26, 40–43, 62, 92–93, 96, 105
Holi, 33, 98
holidays, 33, 40–41, 93–94, 97–98
homosexuality, 85
honor killings, 78
House of the People, 46–48
housing, 76–77
human trafficking, 30–32
hunger, 12, 63, 73
Hyderabad, 65
hygiene, 75–76

I

illegal drugs, 21, 32–33
imports, 52–53, 65, 67–68
independence, 12, 22–23, 37
Independence Day, 40–41
Indian Constitution, 37, 39–40, 42, 44–45, 59, 79, 85, 92, 95–96, 105
Indian Ocean, 14, 28
Indira Gandhi National Open University, 86
Indo-Aryans, 89, 95
Indonesia, 92
Indo-Pakistani Wars, 23–24, 26
industrialization, 9, 12, 56, 62

industries, 6, 12–13, 53, 64
inequality, 41, 70, 72–73, 78, 81–82, 84–87, 91–92
infanticide, 70, 85, 91–92
 See also Beti Bachao, Beti Padhao
information technology, 64–65
insurgency. *See* terrorism
International Men and Gender Equality Survey, 78
Internet access, 71, 81–82
iron, 6, 12, 53, 67
Islam, 7, 14, 22–23, 34, 63, 89, 92, 94, 98, 102, 105

J

Jainism, 97
Jaipur, 83
journalism, 82
judicial branch, 48–49

K

Kannada (language), 89
Kanpur, 83
Kashmir, 14, 18–19, 22–24, 28, 30, 32–34, 92, 106
Kerala, 77
Khan, Abdul Qadeer, 27
kidnapping, 31, 78
 See also human trafficking
Kolkata. *See* Calcutta
Kovind, Ram Nath, 46

L

labor force, 9, 31, 53, 56–59
languages, 14, 49, 54, 82, 88–89, 95–96
legal system, 36–37, 42
legislative branch, 36–38, 40, 45–46
life expectancy, 71, 90
Line of Control, 33
literacy, 13, 43, 60, 71, 79–80
Lok Sabha, 46–48

M

Mahabharata, 85
Mahatma Gandhi, 20, 22, 40–42, 54, 105
Maithili (language), 89
Malayalam (language), 89
malnutrition, 73
Marathi (language), 89

markets, 57–59, 98–99
marriage, 31–32, 78, 85, 91
 See also wedding trade
Mawlid, 98
McMahon Line, 25
media, 71, 82–83
military, 18, 21–28, 33–34, 38
Millennium Developmental Goals, 73
mining, 6, 12–13, 53, 67
minorities, 15, 31
 See also inequality
Missile Technology Control Regime, 29
Mizoram, 93
Modi, Narendra, 19, 45, 106
monetary policy, 54–55
monsoons, 62, 74, 84
mortality rate, 13, 19, 61, 71, 84
Mother Teresa, 15
movies, 82, 96, 99
Mughal Empire, 7
Muhammad, 98
Mumbai, 9, 15, 53, 55, 66, 70, 72, 76–77, 83
murder, 35, 91
Myanmar, 31

N

Nagaland, 77
Narayanan, K. R., 85
narcotics, 32–33
National Congress Party, 43
natural gas, 6, 12, 68
Nehru, Jawaharlal, 26, 40, 45
Nepal, 28, 54
New Delhi, 37, 48
newspapers, 82
Non-Aligned Movement, 26
nonviolence, 20, 40–41
North Atlantic Treaty Organization (NATO), 26, 29, 34
nuclear energy, 68
Nuclear Suppliers Group, 29
nuclear weapons, 14, 25–29, 105
nutrition, 73

O

Obama, Barack, 47
obesity, 71

Odia (language), 89
oil, 6, 12, 53, 65–67
One Belt One Road policy, 28
opium, 21, 32–33
Organization for Economic Co-operation and Development (OCED), 59

P
Pakistan, 7–8, 12, 14, 19, 22–26, 30, 32, 46, 92, 95
parliament, 42, 46–48, 103
per capita income, 53, 56
petroleum, 6, 53, 68
pharmaceuticals, 21, 53
plutonium, 26
political parties, 42–44, 62, 97
politics, 14, 36–51
pollution, 15–16, 19, 66, 68, 83–84
population, 8–9, 15, 56, 63–64, 74, 77, 88–90
 See also gender imbalance; sex ratio
poverty, 12–14, 19, 43, 53, 56–61, 73, 77, 79
precious gems, 13, 53, 68
precious metals, 13, 52, 67–68
president, 38, 44–45, 48
prime minister, 26, 38, 42, 44–46
prisons, 49, 78
prostitution, 32
Punjab (region), 94
Punjabi (language), 89

Q
QR Video
 labor struggles, 61
 learn about a geographical feature, 10
 life in slums, 78
 Mahatma Gandhi, 42
 population growth, 90
 prostitution in India, 32

R
radio, 83
Rajya Sabha, 46, 48
Ramadan, 98

rape, 19, 35
Raxaul, 61
recent headlines, 19
religion, 6, 14, 85, 89, 92
 See also individual religions
reproduction, 61, 63–64
Republic Day, 37, 41
Reserve Bank of India (RBI), 54–55
 See also banking
rupee, 54
Russia, 27, 29–30, 34, 52
 See also BRICS

S
safety, 77–78
sanctions, 28, 103
sanitation, 19, 61, 71, 74–77
Sanskrit (language), 54
Security Council (UN), 16, 29–30
 See also United Nations (UN)
sex ratio, 32, 89, 91
Siddhartha Gautama, 105
Sikh Empire, 94
Sikhism, 63, 89, 92, 94–95, 98
Silk Road, 28, 54
silver, 13, 67
Sino-Indian War, 25–26, 46, 105
slavery, 31
slums, 9, 59–60, 71, 77, 85
social mobility, 84
South Africa, 38, 52
 See also BRICS
spending, 14, 21, 26–27, 33–34, 38
Sri Lanka, 28
St. Patrick's Church, 94
steel, 12, 53, 59
Supreme Court, 45, 48–49
Sustainable Developmental Goals, 73

T
Taj Mahal, 94
Tamil (language), 89
television, 82–83
Telugu (language), 89

terrorism, 7, 14, 21, 28–29, 34–35
textiles, 53, 64–65
Thomas the Apostle, 93
Tibet, 25
toilets, 75–76
tolerance, 14, 85–87
torture, 35
trade, 21, 26–27, 52, 67–68
 See also economy
traffic, 15, 83
Trafficking in Persons Report, 31
transportation, 68, 72
treaties, 26–27

U
undesirables, 31, 77, 79, 84
United Kingdom (UK), 27, 29, 39
United Nations (UN), 16, 24, 29–30, 73
 See also Security Council (UN)
United States (US), 26–29, 34, 39, 68, 73
Uniting for Consensus, 30
universities, 86–87
Urdu (language), 89

V
Vaisakhi, 62, 98
Vedas, 33, 93, 105
violence, 19, 35, 77–78, 92
voting, 36–39, 42–48

W
wars, 22–24
 See also individual wars
water, 12, 16, 60, 71, 74–75
wedding trade, 32
 See also human trafficking; marriage
Well-Being Index, 79
women, 14, 19, 31–32, 47, 60, 71, 73, 75, 78, 80–82, 85, 90–92
 See also abuse; Beti Bachao, Beti Padhao
World Bank, 12, 80

Nations in the News: INDIA

Author's Biography

David Wilson has a bachelor's degree in history from Miami University and a graduate degree in history from the University of Cincinnati. His writings on history have been published by educational institutes like Norwich University, Peregrine Academics, and Study.com. He lives in Denver.

Credits

Cover

Top (left to right): Aji Jayachandran/Dreamstime; SumanBhaumik/Shutterstock; ferrantraite/iStock
Middle (left to right): William Cushman/Shutterstock; SoumenNath/iStock; szefei/Shutterstock
Bottom (left to right): Juliamilberger/Dreamstime; Mukulbanerjee/Dreamstime; joeravi/iStock

Interior

1, turtix/Shutterstock; 6, Steve Allen/Shutterstock; 8, ImagesofIndia/Shutterstock; 9, sladkozaponi/Shutterstock; 10, Maksimilian/Shutterstock; 11, CRS Photo/Shutterstock; 13, Yury Birukov/Shutterstock; 16, diy13/Shutterstock; 18, Vladimir Melnik/Dreamstime; 21, Angelo Giampiccolo/Shutterstock; 22, Egasit Mullakhut/Shutterstock; 23, indianarmy.nic.in/Wikimedia Commons; 27, Antônio Milena (Abr)/Wikimedia Commons; 29, Yudh Abhyas/Wikimedia Commons; 30, Alarax/Shutterstock; 31, Arindam Banerjee/Dreamstime; 33, pilesasmiles/iStock; 37, CRS Photo/Shutterstock; 38, code6d/iStock; 39, Saikat Paul/Shutterstock; 41, CRS Photo/Shutterstock; 43, arindambanerjee/Shutterstock; 45, Nisarg Lakhmani/Dreamstime; 46, Vasilis Ververidis/Dreamstime; 47 (UP), The White House/Wikimedia Commons; 47 (LO), Saikat Paul/Shutterstock; 48, TK Kurikawa/Shutterstock; 50, Prathyush Thomas/Wikimedia Commons; 53, Yavuz Sariyildiz/Shutterstock; 54, prabhat kumar verma/Shutterstock; 55, Saikat Paul/Shutterstock; 57, JeremyRichards/Shutterstock; 58, Don Mammoser/Shutterstock; 59, Hari Mahidhar/Shutterstock; 60, Sharad Raval/Shutterstock; 61, Travel Stock/Shutterstock; 62, Nikhil Gangavane/Dreamstime; 63, may numpetch/Shutterstock; 65, arun sambhu mishra/Shutterstock; 66, AzmanMD/Shutterstock; 67, knyazevfoto/Shutterstock; 71, yavuzsariyildiz/iStock; 72, Snehal Jeevan Pailkar/Shutterstock; 74, Travel Stock/Shutterstock; 75, yavuzsariyildiz/iStock; 76, ertyo5/iStock; 77, SNEHIT/Shutterstock; 79, Saikat Paul/Shutterstock; 80, Meinzahn/iStock; 81, Radiokukka/iStock; 82, Saurav022/Shutterstock; 86, Radiokukka/iStock; 89, ferrantraite/iStock; 90, paulprescott72/iStock; 91, Nisangha/iStock; 93, Rudra Narayan Mitra/Shutterstock; 94 (UP), JeremyRichards/Shutterstock; 94 (LO), Komar/Shutterstock; 95, Prabhjit S. Kalsi/Shutterstock; 96, Pratik Panda/Dreamstime; 97, air420/iStock; 98 (UP), BDphoto/iStock; 98 (LO), Nikada/iStock; 99, BDphoto/iStock

 Nations in the News: